Entertaining ANGELS

SANDY HOPE STEWART

LUCIDBOOKS

Entertaining Angels

Copyright © 2025 by Sandy Hope Stewart

Published by Lucid Books in Houston, TX

www.LucidBooks.com

All rights reserved. No part of this publication may be reproduced, stored in a retrieval system, or transmitted in any form by any means, electronic, mechanical, photocopy, recording, or otherwise, without the prior permission of the publisher, except as provided for by USA copyright law.

Unless otherwise indicated, scripture quotations are taken from the American Standard Version (ASV): American Standard Version, public domain.

Scripture quotations marked (TLB) are taken from The Living Bible copyright © 1971. Used by permission of Tyndale House Publishers, Carol Stream, Illinois 60188. All rights reserved.

ISBN: 978-1-63296-830-2
eISBN: 978-1-63296-831-9

Special Sales: Most Lucid Books titles are available in special quantity discounts. Custom imprinting or excerpting can also be done to fit special needs. Contact Lucid Books at Info@LucidBooks.com

*For God, always my deepest desire,
and for my children,
who have loved me well.*

Contents

Prologue 1

Part 1: Summer 1966 5

Part 2: Summer 1967 65

Part 3: Summer 1968 163

Part 4: Spring 1969 233

Epilogue 257

Post Epilogue 262

Acknowledgments 263

Prologue

**July 2023:
Office of Bradley J. Holcomb,
Doctor of Psychology**

Rebekah Lang thinks about everything. Her husband always said she thought way too much. Of course, he would have said that. Most of the time he was content thinking about nothing. How does a person think of nothing anyway? Nothing is something if you're thinking about it. She did have to admit though, thinking about everything can be so very exhausting.

As she enters what is, in her estimation, a superfluously large waiting area for a therapist's office, she pauses . . .

Isn't privacy the number one consideration in counseling? And the doubts, once again, unfold. I don't even know why I'm here. I should have canceled. I shouldn't have even made the stupid appointment.

She considers walking out, even though she's the only one in the large room at the moment. But the therapist is standing inside an open doorway a few feet in front of her, gesturing for her to please come in. She assumes the "please" part because he seems so very polite and professional.

Although Rebekah has moved on from any thought of the waiting room size, the first thing he says to her is, "I try to let my clients know ahead of time that I am in a temporary office, and they will never see anyone else in the waiting room with them. I schedule appointments far enough apart to maintain privacy. I mention it now in case I forgot before."

"Of course." *That's right. He did say something about a borrowed office.*

"Dr. Holcomb." He held out his hand. "It's good to meet you."

"Nice to meet you too." *I know he is somewhat younger than me, but he looks considerably younger than I imagined. Why is it that men almost always seem to age more gracefully than women?*

Since joining the "septuagenarian club" just a few weeks prior, Rebekah had become a bit obsessed with aging.

The doctor invites her to sit as he makes his way to a chair in front of her. She settles herself on the exceptionally comfortable couch. *I should ask him what brand this couch is. I could use a new one.*

Her stomach quivers, and she forces a smile, but no words come. She has no idea what to say.

"Tell me a bit about yourself, Mrs. Lang, and why you have come today."

"Oh, please, call me Rebekah. I mean, if that's okay."

A genuine-looking smile appears on the doctor's face. "Sure, Rebekah. I can do that. Now, what brings you in today?"

"I uh . . . I," she stutters. "I don't really know why I'm here, or why I even made this appointment." She takes a deep breath and glances up at Dr. Holcomb.

He gives an encouraging nod.

"I'm sure you have clients who need your time more than I do." Rebekah stands and extends her hand for a goodbye shake. "I'm really sorry for wasting your time."

Prologue

Dr. Holcomb rises and cups her hand in both of his. "Well, Rebekah, you're paying for forty-five minutes anyway, so why not get your money's worth? And I can assure you that neither my time nor yours will be wasted."

She appreciates his assurance, but Rebekah is still not convinced. "I am so sorry, but I should go . . ." She attempts to tug her hand out of his.

His voice, soft and calming, interrupts Rebekah. "Just one session. We're already here and you've already paid."

Struck by his warmth and swayed by his logic, she sits back down, reminding herself that, just like those of a client and attorney, communication between a licensed psychologist and patient are protected by law. She also reminds herself that she made sure he is, in fact, licensed by the state of North Carolina.

After a few seconds of silence, which, surprisingly, Rebekah doesn't find uncomfortable at all, the doctor begins again. "Have you ever seen a therapist before, Rebekah?"

"No, I've never even considered it," she lies, looking down at her hands while picking at her cuticles. She did not lie about the "no" part but about the "never considered it" part. Truth is, she'd thought about it for years.

"I'm not sure why I'm here. I almost canceled a few times."

"And yet, here you are." He offers another gentle smile.

Another few silent seconds pass as he waits for her response.

Rebekah holds his gaze. "I killed my best friend," Rebekah whispered. As he absorbs her words, she notices for the first time the kind doctor's beautiful green eyes.

Part 1:
Summer 1966

Saturday, July 9, 1966

"Where The Boys Are"

They were in the happiest of all happy places: Myrtle Beach, South Carolina. Stifling hot, horribly humid, crazy crowded, beautiful, wonderful Myrtle Beach. The waves and the sounds of kids playing drowned out their own squeals as Rebekah gingerly skipped across the blistering sand, her best friend trying to keep up.

"Tell me why we aren't wearing our flip-flops." yelled Pammy. They both knew the answer to that question. If the trip was delayed, it would not be on them. Beach bags had been packed days ahead; bathing suits had been slept in the night before. They'd held the bags in their laps the entire drive from Rebekah's home in Northwest Raleigh.

Flip flops had been kicked off before the car started moving and could have landed anywhere from the back seat to the very back of the station wagon, where they would stay until the girls had, or took, the time to retrieve them. And now was not that time although, in retrospect, it most certainly should have been.

Pamela—nicknamed Pammy by Rebekah, because, well, she had nicknames for all her favorite people (and Pamela Rose Daniels was pretty much her most favorite)—just laughed at her own question. Rebekah and Pammy had been coming to the beach with Rebekah's family since they were in fourth grade. But everything about this year felt different to Rebekah. They were high schoolers—fifteen years old—and with so much more freedom to come and go as they pleased, even more than last summer. In so many ways this felt like her first ever beach vacation.

They weren't as shy around boys anymore either. Well, Rebekah wasn't as shy anymore. Pammy, on the other hand, was still a bit awkward with them. And boys were everywhere. Rebekah watched a group of them watching Pammy and her as they scurried toward the cooler, wet sand.

Without collaboration, the girls stopped at the same spot and spread their oversized towels in the sand. While Pammy dug through the bag for the baby oil, Rebekah fidgeted with the transistor radio until she moved the dial, ever so slowly, past the static and picked up "Surfin' Safari." Immediately they slathered themselves with the oil and fell back in total abandonment to the endorphins filling their carefree minds. At least Rebekah assumed Pammy did the same as her. She didn't look to check. Instead, she reveled in her new knowledge of endorphins.

Rebekah rolled over to her tummy, looking around at her fellow beach lovers, breathing in the salty air and singing along. Pammy lay on her back next to Rebekah, quietly glistening in the sun. Rebekah, on the other hand, almost always sang every word, like it was some kind of jinx to stop before the song ended. Halfway through the song, something strange caught her attention. She finished singing with the Beach Boys, mesmerized by what was taking place several yards away and directly in her sight.

"What the heck is that girl doing?" she asked, as much to herself as to Pammy.

"What girl?" Pammy mumbled without opening her eyes.

"You have to turn over and look." Rebekah nudged her shoulder. "She's moving her hands all around, and it looks really weird and kinda cool."

That wasn't enough to pique Pammy's curiosity or coax her to roll over, but Rebekah kept watching. She figured the two people with the girl must be her parents. She obviously wasn't a teenager yet. Teens never sat with their parents. Especially at the beach.

Losing interest, and with the sun beating down on her back, Rebekah was too sleepy to keep her eyes open or her head propped up, so she rolled over onto her back. She started harmonizing with the Mamas and the Papas' "I Saw Her Again" but drifted off before the second stanza. At some point she woke up just long enough to turn over and unnecessarily apply a coat of Coppertone oil. She took a deep breath of the intoxicating scent and let herself drift back off.

She was startled awake when seawater lapped over her feet and ankles. Pammy jumped up too. Although a bit shocking, the seawater was welcome against their burning skin, enticing the girls into the waves. Tossing her towel and the radio far away from the rising tide, Rebekah glanced around but didn't see the girl and her companions. Maybe she would see them again tomorrow and figure out what the hand-jiving was all about.

As they ran full speed into the waves, Rebekah caught sight of the group of boys, just to the right of them. Again, she was keenly aware of them watching her watching them. She was glad she decided to wear her favorite two-piece bathing suit. She knew she looked good in it and loved the aqua color that made her blue eyes even bluer.

"Pammy! Pammy," she yelled over the wind and surf. "They're here."

When Pammy didn't answer, Rebekah pushed through the water to catch up with her and yelled even louder, "Pammy, they're here."

"Why are you yelling? Who's here?"

"The boys," Rebekah, a bit frustrated at this point, screamed even louder, jerking her head in their direction.

"You talkin' about us?" A grinning boy made his way over to them, and Rebekah thought he was the cutest guy she'd ever seen, except for Mark. But she didn't want to think about Mark right now. He was back home and was her back-home boyfriend, absolutely not her beach boyfriend. It was important to keep them separated.

"No," Rebekah hurriedly answered before Pammy had time to admit that he was right. Pammy didn't understand the importance of the "keep them guessing game," no matter how many times Rebekah tried to explain it to her. Pammy was just Pammy, and she didn't know—nor did she care to learn—how to play games. She thought it was the same as lying, which it clearly was not.

All of which was a moot point since it was clear to Rebekah from his broadening smile that the boy, who was as cute as Mark, if not cuter—she reminded herself to stop thinking about Mark—already knew it was them she was talking about.

"I'm Johnny." He continued smiling while bobbing up and down. "These goofballs are Hank, Greg, and David." Each boy shyly raised a hand out of the water as they were introduced.

Rebekah thought they were all kinda cute, well except for Hank. So, it was a bit surprising seeing Pammy—whom she'd almost forgotten was even there—staring and smiling at him. And Hank returned the same to her.

Rebekah turned to introduce themselves when a wave crashed over Pammy's head. A heartbeat later, she popped back up, laughing. For several minutes, it was all any of them could do to stay above the water's surface as the waves came one right after another. Rebekah was getting nervous about the bigger and stronger waves that were starting to get the better of her. Her legs and arms were getting tired. Being a strong swimmer was no asset when it came to undertow, and she could feel the retreating waves working against her efforts to move toward shore. Just as she turned to tell Pammy to move that way too, Pammy disappeared. She waited a few seconds, but Pammy didn't reappear. Rebekah swam farther out. She caught a glimpse of Pammy and grabbed her arm. Pammy fought against Rebekah's grip, gasped for breath, and went under again, pulling Rebekah with her. Rebekah's mind raged. Had the boys already headed into shore? Or had they been pulled under too?

Rebekah's yell for help was muffled by the sound of the crashing waves. She frantically looked for the boys and Pammy but saw no one.

Suddenly, Johnny was back next to Rebekah, gasping for air. "I don't see your friend," he yelled. "The current started pulling me out too. Come on. Let's go back." He gripped Rebekah's arm and pulled her toward the shore, but she fought off his attempts, just as Pammy had done with her moments before. She knew she couldn't do anything but couldn't leave Pammy out there alone.

Pammy appeared for the third time, and again Rebekah grabbed her arm, only to feel it slip away as Pammy slowly and calmly sank out of sight. Rebekah heaved. Her lungs felt like they were about to explode. She gulped as much air as she could and dove under in one last attempt to save her best friend.

Pammy was nowhere to be found. Rebekah, knowing that she was on the verge of drowning, popped back up, breathing in what felt like every bit of available oxygen. Unable to think straight, feeling sick and, at the same time, like she was having some sort of out-of-body experience, Rebekah turned one last time, hoping against hope that she would see her best friend coming toward her.

What she saw made her question her own sanity. A strange and rather large man carried Pammy, moving quickly through the water to the shoreline. Was it real or was she hallucinating? Although it made no sense, she decided it must be real and raced toward the shore. The man had already administered CPR by the time the rest of them made it to shore. The five of them staggered up to where the stranger was kneeling next to Pammy as she spurted up water, coughed, and took one deep, gasping breath. And, surreal as it was, after coughing several more times and breathing in a few seemingly painful breaths, Pammy met Rebekah's gaze. She was shaken up, dazed, and confused, but otherwise fine.

Hank ran off while the three other boys stared down at her, saying nothing at all. Rebekah went on and on to Pammy about how she scared her so bad. "I thought you were gone. I'd never be able to live without you." She kept going on and on and on about how bad it was for her—Rebekah.

"Who was that man?" Johnny asked.

Rebekah glanced around. He'd left without saying a word and without any of them thanking him.

Hank rejoined the group and wrapped a towel around Pammy's shoulders.

"I have no idea who he is, but that man is my hero," Rebekah replied.

No one had to ask whom she spoke of, though she imagined they'd all been wondering about the man who showed up out of nowhere and carried Pammy out of the ocean.

The six of them sat silently in a circle. Rebekah allowed herself to briefly consider whether she accidentally pulled Pammy under in her effort to save her. Physically shaking her head, she mentally shook away the thought of such a thing.

Johnny stood up. One by one, the other boys followed suit. Pammy, still looking like she was in a state of shock, remained seated. Rebekah sat with her but turned her attention to the boys. To one boy in particular and for the first time, she noticed Johnny's beautiful green eyes.

"So, do you . . . think you'll be up for . . . going to the pavilion tonight?" asked Johnny. Even if he was thinking it might be inappropriate to start planning the evening right after one of them almost drowned, Rebekah dismissed his reservations, and she didn't need to ask which pavilion he was talking about. Everybody knew that "The Pavilion" was the big one down at the main strand of Myrtle Beach. They also knew that the much smaller one at this beach was the pavilion they all loved and considered their very own hangout.

Rebekah jumped up. "Oh, yeah! For sure. You?" *Calm down, silly girl.* She had to put the brakes on her obvious eagerness. That wouldn't keep him guessing.

"Yep, we usually head up there about seven. We'll watch for you. Uh, if you want us to."

"Sounds good," Rebekah answered, trying not to sound too excited this time.

Hank looked at Pammy and mumbled, "Glad you're okay."

Pammy looked up for the first time and gave him a soft smile. He beamed back at her and practically skipped away, as the four of them turned and walked in the opposite direction from which the girls had come.

When they were almost out of sight, Johnny turned and ran back to the girls. "What are your names?" he asked, panting and bending at the waist, hands on his knees.

"I'm Rebekah, and this is Pammy," she offered. *And you have the most amazing smile I've ever seen.*

Johnny turned and sprinted back to where the others waited. After they walked a few more feet, he turned around and ran right back again. "Where are you staying?"

Rebekah gave him a vague idea because she had only a vague idea. She knew where the cottage was, but she had no clue what street they were staying on or the names of any of the ones between here and there. It must have been enough for Johnny.

"I know exactly where that is." He turned and ran back to the others. Rebekah watched them until they were almost completely out of sight.

She then decided that Pammy was good to go and gathered their belongings. Too much adrenaline or excitement or something ran through her veins to sit still.

"Let's head home to eat and get ready for the night."

Pammy was very quiet the whole way back, but Rebekah never stopped talking. "Man, I'm starving. Oh, my gosh, Pammy, did you see how beautiful Johnny's eyes are? What should we wear tonight? Remember the first time we went to the pavilion? We were just kids then." Rebekah barely noticed that Pammy was quieter even than her usual self.

Climbing the few steps onto the screen porch of the cottage, Rebekah clutched Pammy's arm. "We cannot tell my parents that you almost drowned."

Pammy crinkled her brow. "Why not?"

Rebekah's mouth dropped open. "Are you kidding? They wouldn't let us go back down to the beach alone anymore if they knew what happened."

Pammy, being Pammy, accepted the explanation in her usual easy-going way. But Rebekah knew that Pammy probably thought it was a bit like lying—clearly, it was not.

୫ଓ

Part 1: Summer 1966

"Good Vibrations"

Rebekah's already blonde hair had lightened a bit from just one day in the sun. Her naturally pale face was slightly sunburned but not painful. She turned from the mirror and glanced down. Her legs, chest, and stomach, on the other hand, were very much sunburned. But one last check in the mirror boosted her confidence enough to help her forget about her burning skin.

The sundress, white cotton covered in small yellow daisies, was her favorite, and the yellow sandals her mother got to go with it were perfect. Her mom was cool. She made sure that Rebekah liked something before buying it. So many of her friends were always talking about the fights they had with their mothers over the stuff they wore. But Rebekah's mother got it. She even let her wear mascara and a little blush, although her mother insisted on calling it rouge—with a bit of a French accent. But Rebekah didn't need any more color on her cheeks that night.

Pammy wore a pink polka-dot mini skirt and white sleeveless blouse. Her beautiful long legs showed off in the white open-toed slip-ons, but they also brought unwanted attention to her large feet and long toes. Every time Pammy mentioned it, Rebekah reassured her that feet were everyone's least attractive feature, without mentioning that she considered her own feet to be kinda cute. Pammy's short dark hair and brown eyes matched her dark complexion. Pammy did not wear make-up that night. In fact, she never did.

The two girls were opposite in almost every way. After so many years of being practically attached at the hip, they figured the saying that opposites attract could certainly apply to best friends too.

As the two made their way to the pavilion, Rebekah began to rattle off the list of songs she wanted to play on the jukebox. Fighting the urge to sing every word, she allowed herself to sing only the first line of each one. Pammy stayed quiet.

Rebekah was used to this with her best friend. She didn't feel the need to sing every word to every song like Rebekah did—or even a first line, for that matter. After a bunch of song titles and first-line renditions, Rebekah took a breath and glanced at Pammy.

"Yellow Submarine," Pammy suggested after fifteen whole seconds of silence.

Rebekah belted out the first line. She couldn't understand how anyone could talk about a song without actually singing it—at least part of it. Pammy, however, rarely knew many of the words. But she still loved the songs. That made no sense at all to Rebekah, but Pammy was Pammy, and she didn't need to know the words to like the songs. Rebekah needed to know every word—whether she liked the song or not.

The sound of the music and vibrations of the beat reached them long before they entered the beloved structure. "Summer in the City" had just started, and, per usual, Rebekah began singing along with The Lovin' Spoonful. She looked around, thinking how refreshing it was that something so special, like the pavilion, looked the same every summer. While so many other things in life seemed to be changing faster than she could keep up—there was talk about a war far, far away, among other things—she couldn't help but notice that at least the rustic, open-air pavilion with the wood-plank dance floor and trusty jukebox were a mainstay. She also picked up another, somewhat familiar, voice. She turned to see Johnny leaning against the wooden railing closest to the ocean view. The breeze was blowing the part in his dark—almost black—hair to the wrong side. He didn't skip one word of the song as he slipped his fingers through his hair to set the part back in its proper place, inviting a butterfly convention to convene in Rebekah's stomach.

Their eyes locked, as she came face to face with him, both of them continuing to sing the entire song. Rebekah felt her knees go weak, this time noticing his long dark eyelashes. *Why did boys even have long eyelashes? They don't need them. They didn't even care. They were usually just a nuisance to them. At least that's how the boy, who shall not be thought of, acts.*

"You came." Johnny smiled, his green eyes sparkling.

"Of course. I told you I would." Rebekah flipped a lock of hair off her shoulder.

"Thought you might change your mind, is all." He shrugged.

Fully aware that she was in danger of failing at her own motto to "keep them guessing," Rebekah took a step back, sighed, and perused the area as if she was already getting bored. Pammy might be well aware that Rebekah was, and had always been, boy crazy, but Johnny didn't need to know.

Rebekah couldn't deny it. When she was three years old, she had her first boyfriend. Of course, two-year-old Brent had no idea that an older woman was interested in him. The romance ended almost as soon as it started when his older sister started pulling Rebekah's white-blonde pigtails. Brent just wasn't worth that kind of trouble. By age six her sights were set on much older men, like Sky King and Roy Rogers. But in fifth grade, she had her first real crush on a boy. He sat at the front of the class, and she sat two seats behind him. He had dark hair and green eyes. He didn't seem particularly interested in her, but his best friend thought Rebekah was the cutest girl on the planet and asked his friend to be a go-between for passing notes back and forth to her. The first note was a multiple choice, requiring her to circle the correct answer.

Do you like me? 1. YES 2. NO 3. MAYBE

Of course she had to circle "MAYBE." It was the only way to keep some form of communication between her and the cute wingman. Even if it did give false hope to the not-so-cute guy. She could not remember how long the hoax continued before all three of them moved on to other quests, such as jump rope contests for her and arm wrestling for them.

Someone put another quarter in the jukebox, and "It's in His Kiss" filled the pavilion. Rebekah didn't know anything about that since she hadn't even kissed a boy yet—and wasn't in any hurry to do so either. Not with Johnny or with the boy she didn't want to think about. But that didn't keep her from singing along. She may be boy crazy, but she wasn't ready to go there. Not just yet anyway. But she was thinking about it an awful lot lately.

She turned to look for Pammy and felt a bit of panic when she didn't see her. For the first time since her friend's near drowning, the memory of the day's earlier event rushed through her mind. About the time she was able to focus again, she heard Pammy talking to Johnny. She turned her head around to see Pammy lunging into Johnny's arms. What the heck?

Rebekah stopped mid-song. "Pammy, what in the world are you thinking?"

Pammy not only didn't answer her, but she went completely limp, slumping further into Johnny's arms.

"Are the Stars Out Tonight?"

"What happened?" Rebekah's mother insisted on knowing why the girls came home so early.

"Pammy wasn't feeling well, so we just decided to come back and go to bed early," Rebekah explained.

"Pammy, can I get you something? Is it your tummy? Or a headache?" Mama asked.

"I'm fine, Mrs. Lang, honest. The first day in the sun always gets to me." Pammy shot a glance at Rebekah as if to say, I don't like it, but I will keep our secret.

"I'll get you both big glasses of water. And, Pammy, you let me know if you start feeling badly again. Even if it's in the middle of the night, okay?"

"She will, Mama, but I think she just needs to get some sleep." Rebekah needed the conversation to end before Pammy said anything else. She didn't want her spilling the beans about almost drowning that afternoon and then fainting at the pavilion. That information had the potential to ruin the rest of their week. Her parents were liable to pack them up and head for home before they even had time to get a tan, much less hang out with the boys.

As soon as her mother returned with the glasses of water, Rebekah grabbed Pammy's arm and whisked her to the bedroom where they could talk.

"Okay, spill. What happened?"

Pammy played with the hem of her skirt. "I didn't eat anything before we went. That's probably why I fainted." Pink flushed her cheeks.

"Girl, don't do that." Rebekah rolled her eyes and popped up to get her pajamas on. Pammy followed suit, although she didn't so much pop up as gently stood.

Rebekah fell back on the bed, twirling a strand of hair. Johnny was so dreamy. She couldn't wait to see him again.

Pammy sat next to her, remaining her usual, quiet self.

Oh! "You need food," Rebekah declared before hopping off the bed again and racing out of the room.

She grabbed some leftover potato salad and a piece of cheese for Pammy and a cold hot dog for herself. She chuckled out loud at the oxymoron of a cold hot dog. That was the first time she got to use the word *oxymoron* since learning it last year.

"Thanks," Pammy said as she accepted the food.

"Sure."

Rebekah lifted the hot dog to take her first bite, and something tapped on the window.

Rebekah peeked around the flimsy curtain to see all four of the boys standing there. She tried to raise the window, but it was stuck. Pammy came over, and between the two of them they managed to raise it about six inches. They sat on the floor by the window, and the boys came up so close that Rebekah could smell Johnny's minty breath. Becoming self-conscious of her own, she grabbed her water and drank about half of the glass, hoping it would wash any yuck down. And then she said a little prayer, just in case.

"How did you even find our cottage?" she whispered.

"Well, you gave us enough of an idea of where it was and what it looked like, so it was pretty easy to find," answered one of the boys, Greg or David—Rebekah couldn't remember who was who between them. Besides, it was the first time either of them even spoke.

"So," Hank whispered, "are you okay?" His eyes focused on Pammy.

"I'm okay. I think I just needed to eat something."

"That's good," he added, sheepishly.

"We just wanted to be sure. Do you think you'll be at the same place on the beach tomorrow?" Johnny asked.

"Absolutely," Rebekah answered, without a thought as to how Pammy would be feeling. She had to feel better; their vacation depended on it. Their love lives depended on it.

The boys said their goodbyes and snuck away.

They never had boys come to their bedroom window before. It was like *Rebel Without a Cause* or *A Summer Place*. It was exciting and a little dangerous—after all, the girls were in their baby doll pajamas for goodness' sake.

Rebekah decided they should eat and go right to sleep so they could get up early and be on the beach when the boys showed up.

Sunday, July 10, 1966

"Johnny Angel"

The girls were up and in their bathing suits before Rebekah's parents were even awake.

Rebekah had figured she would have to wake Pammy up and then rush out, so she snuck out of the bedroom, quickly and quietly to pack some breakfast snacks—well, probably not actually snacks intended for breakfast—but who cared? She woke her friend the same way she usually did—with a serenade. Rebekah began softly singing, "Hanky Panky." After repeating the first line several times with no indication that Pammy was waking, she leaned over right up against her ear and tried again, singing the entire first line.

Pammy's left eye cracked open, and a slight smile appeared. "I see what you did there—HANKy Panky," she said in her gravelly morning voice. It was all the motivation Pammy needed to jump up and hit the floor running. Obviously, she was feeling much better. And so was Rebekah—summer vacation week 1966 was still on.

As they made their way through the small, overly furnished living room and onto the screen porch, Rebekah handed the cooler of snacks to Pammy as she grabbed two of the floats. Being careful not to let the screen door slam, they sprinted down the concrete steps, discovering the abandoned flip flops at the bottom of the last step. *Awe, Mama and Daddy knew we would need them.* They ran all the way to their usual spot without saying a word. They were on a mission, and the mission was a complete success.

"Same bat time, same bat station," Pammy chuckled as they spread their fresh beach towels on the sand. "Do you like that show?"

"No," Rebekah barked. "But I do watch it when I'm babysitting because there's nothing else on Saturday night to watch. Do you?"

"I do," Pammy replied. "I think both Batman and Robin are the cutest."

"Well, I do agree with you on that, but not as cute as Johnny."

Pammy turned to face Rebekah. "Don't you feel bad about liking Johnny while Mark's back home thinking you like him?"

Rebekah, considering for a second that maybe Pammy was right, stopped herself from doing so. "It's not that I don't like Mark. But he's not here, and he'll never even know there was a Johnny." She gazed straight into Pammy's innocent wide eyes. "Right? He'll never know, right?"

She already knew Pammy would never say anything, but she wanted to be sure that Pammy knew that she knew. "We're only fifteen years old. Who knows how many more boyfriends we'll have before we're old?"

Pammy couldn't argue with that, not that she would anyway. Pammy was just Pammy, and Pammy did not like disagreements. Rebekah added one more very important point—perhaps the most important point—to her explanation. "Besides," she continued, "I don't even know any Mark songs."

Pammy frowned and lifted her eyebrows. "What does that even mean?"

Rebekah needed only to sing her answer. She sang one song after the other in full, starting with "Johnny Get Angry," followed by "Big Bad John" and ending with the one she had been singing to herself since he first flashed his beautiful smile at her—"Johnny Angel."

Pammy laughed and nodded. "Okay, okay. I get it."

"Sunny Afternoon"

It wasn't even ten o'clock, but the sun was already feeling hot when Rebekah suggested, "Let's go ahead and get in a little time on the floats before the boys get here."

She had no sooner got the words out when a quick glance at Pammy's face confirmed what she suddenly realized was not a very smart idea. Pammy looked like she had just swallowed something gross and was about to throw it right back up. Obviously, the thought of getting back into the ocean was just as sickening.

Rebekah did something she rarely did. "I'm so sorry, Pammy. I shouldn't have suggested it. It's too soon."

Pammy shook her head. "No, I need to get back out there. I can't let fear keep me out of the water forever. I just don't . . . think I'm quite ready."

"Well, Pammy, let's not wait too long. The longer we wait, the harder it will be."

Pammy reached out and squeezed Rebekah's hand. She understood. It was times like this that Pammy and Rebekah shared a rare moment of things that didn't need to be said. Things like they truly were the best of friends, and truly did love each other, no matter their quirks. Even if Rebekah was selfish and self-centered, sometimes . . . well, most of time.

As it turned out, they would not have had time for a quick dip before the boys got there, after all. "Morning, Rebekah. Morning, Pammy," four male voices yelled from behind them.

The girls jumped and screamed, probably just like the boys had hoped they would.

Boys are so fun, thought Rebekah.

By the look on her best friend's face, Rebekah knew Pammy was thinking how weird boys were. They'd had that discussion more than once. They both laughed even heartier than their perpetrators.

None of the boys thought to bring anything to sit on, so for a few awkward minutes, shuffling their feet, they tried to decide what to do. Should they sit in the sand? Should they just head for the waves? Should they just keep walking?

Greg and David grabbed the girls' rafts and made their way out and over the weak waves.

Rebekah watched Johnny survey their space. The towels occupied by the girls were plenty big enough for two. Rebekah hoped he'd join her. Her heart leapt when he nudged Hank and took a seat at the bottom of Rebekah's towel—bright blue with a big yellow sun and the words "Sunny Afternoon." Hank followed suit doing the same on Pammy's green and red striped towel, although not quite as confidently as did Johnny. The fact that they didn't even need a hint from the girls to do so did not go unnoticed by Rebekah.

They hadn't been sitting there very long when Johnny asked, "You want to see something really strange?"

Hank shrugged his shoulders and raised his eyebrows.

"Sure. Where is it?" Rebekah countered, as she glanced around.

"You'll just have to find out, won't you?" He wiggled his eyebrows.

And just like that, without any further discussion, the four of them stood up, gathered their belongings and headed down the beach toward the fishing pier.

☙❧

"Under The Boardwalk"

The pier looked much closer than it was. Once they were close enough to barely make out the figures of folks either bustling back and forth or throwing fishing lines over its sides, Johnny said, "It's way past time for a snack and soda break. What do you think?"

Rebekah wiped a bead of sweat off her forehead. "Thought you'd never ask."

A touch of pink tinged Johnny's cheeks. Rebekah couldn't tell whether it was from the sun or something else. "We planned to stop when we got close to the Dairy Queen. Burgers and fries sound so good."

"But that's way behind us now," Hank added.

Rebekah grinned and held up her bag. "Good thing one of us was responsible and packed more than enough for all of us." She didn't mention that she had not, however, wanted to take time to "make" anything. They laid out the colorful towels and sat, eating potato chips, pretzels, and chocolate chip cookies and sharing Orange Crush from the two bottles she'd included.

It just might have been one of the best "meals" she could remember. Everything tasted even more salty than usual, even the soda, but Rebekah didn't think anything of it, and no one else said anything about it. The strong salty taste that the ocean air brought to everything would not be appreciated anywhere else—but at the beach, it was a staple.

As soon as Rebekah took the first bite of her cookie, something very familiar caught her eye up on the fishing pier. They were too far away to clearly see the faces, but she just knew it had to be them. A man, a woman and a girl. They were doing it again.

"Pammy, that's her. That's them," she burst out.

Pammy didn't respond. Between the crashing waves, voices all around them, and competing transistor music coming from every direction, she seemed to be in some kind of trance. Well, all of that, and the fact that she was completely caught up in every word spoken by Hank. Who knew Hank had so much to say?

"Huh?" she finally responded, her eyes locking with Hank's for a few seconds before looking down and shyly making circles in the sand with her index finger.

Rebekah turned her attention to Johnny, who was looking back and forth from her to the fishing pier through squinted eyes, shrugging his shoulders.

"You guys, look," she went on. "See those three people about half-way down the pier. They're next to the lady in the bright orange floppy hat."

And with that, her mouth fell open and stayed that way for several seconds before she asked, "Does anyone, by chance, have binoculars?" knowing full well that no one did.

That question got Pammy's attention.

Before Pammy could ask Rebekah if she was suffering from heat-stroke, Rebekah whispered, "That's my mother. Oh, my goodness, that . . . is . . . my . . . mother! I have never seen that silly sun hat before, and my mother does not smoke. But I know that's her, and she is definitely smoking."

"And also . . . ," just above a whisper now, she finished what she started to say before the shocking cigarette-smoking realization, "those three people are the ones I saw on the beach yesterday. The ones who were doing exactly what they are doing right now."

"You mean sign language?" asked Johnny. "They're speaking to each other through sign language because at least one of them is deaf."

"How did I not know that?" Rebekah responded, remembering how she loved the book and the movie, *The Miracle Worker*. She still had images of Patty Duke as Helen Keller in her mind. She thought she was the best actress she had ever seen. And *The Patty Duke Show* was one of her absolute favorites ever.

"Maybe I've been suffering from sunstroke since we got here," she continued, "because I also think that man is the one who saved Pammy from drowning."

"This is for sure the craziest beach trip we've ever had," Pammy mused.

"And it's only Sunday," Hank exclaimed.

As the four of them sat staring back and forth between the man who might just be their unsung hero and the middle-aged woman who might just be Rebekah's mother, the woman, who may or may not be Rebekah's mother, used the butt of her cigarette to light up another one.

As if all of that wasn't enough to chew on for quite a while, the next thing blew everything way out of proportion. A man, who was not Rebekah's father, approached the woman with open arms. Rebekah, who was completely unprepared to witness their warm embrace, reached the obvious conclusion that the woman was not her mother after all.

A much-welcomed sigh of relief, followed by a renewed sense of calm brought her back to her senses. She could put that ridiculous idea right out of her mind.

Or could she? Another quick glance brought it all back again. That woman who could not possibly be her mother just might very well be her mother. Or her twin. Just like in *The Patty Duke Show*.

☙ ❧

"Blowin' in the Wind"

Rebekah was baffled. But neither she nor the others were about to make their way up to the folks on the pier. What would they even say? What if the strange man wasn't the stranger who saved Pammy? As for her mother, Rebekah wouldn't even know where to start. The scene had conjured up a lot of questions. Where was her father? Did he know that Mama smoked? Did he care? What other nefarious deeds was her mother up to? Did she really want to know? All too much to think about just then. As curious as she was about all that, and she was very much so, she was just as curious about where Johnny was taking them. She couldn't find any answers in that moment, so she shook off all her questions.

They cleaned up their lunch, gathered up the towels, and continued down the beach, Johnny leading the way once again. Ten minutes later, they were still walking, leaving the pier and its mysterious occupants behind and out of sight. Johnny was giving up nothing in the way of hints. He held his ground through the drilling from the others. Rebekah's legs ached. She was thirsty. Both Pammy and Hank had complained about the same.

They made their way up the wide strand to a vendor cart where each of them bought the biggest flavored ice available. They plopped down right there on the sand. Their crunching on the ice and slurping the fruit flavors was the only thing that broke the silence. The others might have been enjoying the warm breeze and the gentle lapping of the calm waves, but Rebekah was using the quiet time the same way she always did—thinking, thinking, and thinking. One thought led to another and another, and she wished she had paper and pencil with her. Sharing her thoughts with the others as a way to help her remember the important stuff was not an option. They could never understand how and why she thought like she did. She didn't even understand most of the time.

Finally, Johnny announced that they were close to their destination, and the group jumped up, energy levels restored, thirsts quenched, and curious minds ready for the big reveal.

They passed cottage after cottage. Oceanfront cottages, sitting high above the sand, had always fascinated Rebekah. Whether small one-story ones or very big two- and three-story houses, they all stood tall on stilts. As hard as she tried, she could not understand how the narrow pieces of lumber, no matter how many there were, could hold the weight of the cottages. Especially since they were placed in sand. Sand was certainly not the sturdiest surface. But then again, she was no builder or sturdy surfaces expert.

Most of the cottages were, or had been, painted bright colors. Some had signs with the names of the cottages, cute names that meant something to the owners if to no one else. The sand and wind were not friendly to the structures, and many needed repainting. The ones with more than one story featured covered or screened-in porches that ran the full width of the house. As she watched folks sitting in their rocking chairs, sipping on drinks, laughing, and going in and out of the cottages, she found herself wanting to be right there with them. She wondered what the insides of such big places might look like. The cottage her family stayed in was a one-story place that sat several rows back from the beachfront, no stilts—just some cinderblocks to lift it off the ground a bit—and not nearly as inviting as the ones that overlooked the ocean.

She was pulled away from her thoughts when Johnny announced, "It's just up ahead."

Pammy and Hank held expressions that clearly indicated they had no idea what they were supposed to be looking at. Neither did Rebekah, and she suspected her face looked similar to theirs. She raised an eyebrow.

"See that really short white fence that runs all the way down the beach from the top of the dunes to the water?" Johnny pointed to his left with his index finger and moved his finger to the right. "Well, when we get to that fence, you'll see what I'm talking about."

As they approached the fence, they did see what Johnny was talking about, and it made Rebekah feel a bit queasy although she didn't know exactly why.

"That's the Colored Beach. They aren't allowed to come to this side of the fence." A few seconds passed without any conversation, as they stared ahead.

Pammy spoke first. She asked, "Why not?"

Johnny didn't answer.

Rebekah looked at him. "Are we allowed to go to their side?"

"We're allowed to do whatever we want. But whites don't want to do that," he informed her.

"Why not?" Pammy asked again.

Hank spoke up for the first time since they had stopped for a break. "I know why. I mean I kinda know why."

Just as they turned toward him for his answer, a beach ball landed at their feet. Looking up to see where it came from, Rebekah saw a colored boy who looked to be about ten years old, running toward them. He stopped short upon seeing them, his eyes opened wide. He was close enough for Rebekah to notice the slight quiver of his lower lip. He turned to go back when Hank picked up the beach ball and called out to the boy, "Here ya go!" He tossed it back to the other side of the fence.

The boy scooped it up and ran. Was that a faint smile replacing the quiver?

And just like that, they all turned around and began the long trek back to where they started the journey.

It's not as if this was the first time Rebekah had seen a colored person. And certainly not the first time she heard about the separation of whites and coloreds, but this scene brought it home to her in a way that reading about it or hearing about it on the news did not—could not. She never gave any thought—until today—to the reality that colored people enjoyed the same things that white people did.

She was confused. The day had been full of unexpected, unsettling events that brought many thoughts and questions. And now, it had brought something else that she could not quite grasp. As tiresome as her many thoughts and questions could be, this one also brought with it a feeling—she felt fear. Exactly what she was afraid of, she wasn't sure.

The war talk, from which she could easily distance herself; seeing the woman who maybe was or maybe wasn't her mama—but sure looked like her mama; seeing the man who may or may not be the mysterious man who saved Pammy; then seeing another man hugging the woman who may or may not be her mama; and now seeing this weird separation fence . . . It was just all way too much for her—physically, mentally, and emotionally. It made her question the predictable and sensible life she had always known. A life that had been pretty much about her.

Had her life, all fifteen years, been a façade? Was there really a lot more to life than boys and music and vacations? She knew, of course, that there must be way more to life than those things. She had her inkling of that truth when a few of her friends' older brothers or cousins went off to war. But she didn't think it was fair to have to look for answers when there was still so much time to be young and carefree.

Besides, does anyone really have any answers? Certainly not her parents. She was beginning to realize that they were a huge part of her suddenly mixed-up life. That was, if her mama really was a chain-smoker who hugged strange men right there in public and if her daddy really had no clue.

"Walking in the Rain"

"Why did you take us there?" Pammy was the first to speak up after the four of them had walked in silence for quite some time.

Rebekah wasn't ready to voice her myriad of thoughts.

"Because it really bugs me, and I wondered if it would bug you guys too, is all," Johnny's response was immediate and passionate, with a hint of anger in his voice.

After a few minutes of silence, Rebekah spoke up. "I just don't understand it. I've heard that folks say white people in the South don't like colored people, but I don't have any idea why that is." Her eyes filled with tears. "We have a colored lady who comes to our house sometimes. Her name is Vonnie Ella, and she does the ironing. She's nice, super quiet, and she irons everything really good. But nobody talks to her much at all, except for maybe Mama. Maybe if I talk to her, she'll know that not all Southern white people dislike colored people. I just never thought about it before."

Johnny, Pammy, and Rebekah chatted a bit about how scared the little boy looked when he saw them. What must have happened to him or someone he knew for him to be so scared of four white teenagers? Maybe they would feel the same if they came up on a group of colored people. Not because of any reason, just because they didn't trust each other. And they didn't trust each other because they didn't know each other.

"I think I understand it, at least a little bit," Hank said. "I've never told anybody this before, but maybe I should have. Some things are just hard to put into words, you know?" He looked over to see that the three of them were hanging onto his every word.

Rebekah kept her gaze on him. He hadn't said that much at one time the whole day. She got the sense he stayed quiet most of the time.

"Our family comes here every year," Hank continued. "Two summers ago, my brother and I met this kid and hung out every day 'cause we really hit it off. He was funny and told jokes all the time. We didn't think anything of it at the time, but some of his jokes were about colored people. Actually, almost all his jokes were about lots of different people—except never about white Christian people. He told lots of jokes about Jews. He told jokes about Polish people. He called those Pollock jokes. He made fun of Chinese and Japanese people's eyes. Stuff like that.

"My brother and I always laughed because it was so funny the way he told them, but I don't think either one of us had any idea why they were supposed to be funny. Anyway, a couple of days before the end of our vacation, it rained all day. He shows up at our cottage, soaking wet and asks if we want to go to the movie theater with him to see *Stagecoach*. We were just glad to have something to do besides sit around inside all day. The rain let up some, so we took off as fast as we could to the campsite where his family was staying.

"We piled into the station wagon with my brother and me sitting by the windows on each side in the back seat and our friend between us. He had a little sister who sat in the very back with a friend she invited. His mom was in the front, and his dad drove."

Rebekah definitely hadn't heard him talk that much. She wondered if he'd ever said so much at one time before in his life.

No one spoke. She could not imagine where the story was going but had a gut feeling it wasn't anywhere good.

Hank continued. "Okay, so where was I? Oh, yeah, so anyway, and I am not exaggerating either, as soon as his father closed the door and started the car, he started talking about coloreds, except he didn't call them that. He called them the N-word. And again, I am not exaggerating, he did not stop cussing and ranting about "N's" all the way there. And when he saw a colored person along the way he would say . . . the only good "N" is a dead "N" and stuff like that. I was so scared. I'd never been around someone with so much hate spewing from his lips in all my life. I hope I never do again. So, Johnny, you wonder if it bugs me too? You're dang right it bugs me. It bugs the mess out of me!"

Just as he stopped talking, a light rain began to fall. Within minutes, it was coming in sheets from across the ocean. Anyone looking down from one of the beautiful wrap-around porches would have seen four figures walking slowly down the beach, obviously in no hurry to escape the downfall. Truth was, they were only vaguely aware of it at all.

By the time they got to their cottage, Rebekah was soaked to the bone and shivering. She glanced to her side to see Pammy trembling too. Towels and clean clothes eased the shivering that the rain brought but no external comfort could ease the shivers inside brought on by Hank's chilling story.

Monday, July 11, 1966

"You Were On My Mind"

The rain continued through the night, and it was raining still when they awoke. Rebekah was impatiently waiting for the lightning to stop so that they could at least walk up to Dairy Queen for a cone. Something . . . anything to remind her they were still at the beach, her happiest of all happy places.

She and Pammy had been holed up in the bedroom, avoiding any and all contact with "mother" and "father." That's what she decided to call them. Mama and Daddy were way too sentimental for strangers, after all. They were now strangers in this strange world that she could never have imagined before yesterday.

Pammy interrupted Rebekah's thoughts. "What do you think the boys are doing?"

"Maybe they're wondering what we're doing," Rebekah offered.

"I hope so," Pammy answered before Rebekah finished with the same words.

Pammy turned from the window and faced Rebekah. "What are you going to do?"

"About what?"

"About what?" Pammy raised her voice. "About your mama!"

"You mean my mother?"

"Oh, yeah, your mother." Pammy must have forgotten about the change.

Rebekah sat quietly, contemplating Pammy's question. She had been thinking of little else since her eyes popped open that morning, before any light of day had appeared. That always happened to her when she had a lot on her mind. For the life of her, she could not remember what possibly would have weighed so heavily on her leading up to this. Somehow, she knew, though, that she would not be able to forget this. Whatever *this* was. Deep down inside she knew, as much as she wanted to ignore it or pretend it didn't happen, she had to somehow confront her mother about it all. How or when she would do so—she had no idea.

"Hello Muddah, Hello Fadduh"

The girls almost made it out of the cottage undetected—almost. The aroma of bacon gave them just enough pause to stop short of their exit. Just enough time for Rebekah's mother to catch a glimpse of them.

"Where are you going? I just cooked up some bacon. Come. Eat. I know you must have smelled it. My goodness, what have you two been hiding from?"

Rebekah knew when her mother meant business and would not be swayed. Besides it would be a shame to miss out on the warm-from-the-oven honey buns that always accompanied her perfectly crisp bacon. She unnecessarily nudged Pammy's arm and rolled her eyes to say without saying, follow my cue—Pammy always followed her cue.

For the first time since arriving, the four of them sat together in the surprisingly large kitchen. Rebekah looked around the simply decorated kitchen, appreciative of the fact that the walls, which were just as white as the appliances, were bare, but for two pictures—one of three seagulls hovering over the shoreline and one of a young girl walking the same strip with her hands full of seashells. It was her favorite room in the cottage, and that had everything to do with the hardwood table and chairs where they had enjoyed so many of her mother's amazing meals—made all the better by the steamy salt air circulating the kitchen from the lone window.

And just as she was contemplating setting aside any confrontation, she was unexpectedly taken back to an earlier time as she rubbed her finger over the deep scratch on the tabletop. Staring at the scratch, she thought of the seven- or eight-year-old whose world was perfectly perfect in every way.

Or was it?

Her mother had fried bacon that day too. What a strange thing to suddenly remember. That day long ago, why did her mother leave before they'd finished eating? Had she been crying? Why did her father use his knife to make that scratch? Was she recalling a memory or remembering a bad dream?

"Rebekah Louise!" her mother, all but screaming, brought her back to the present. "What are you thinking? I've been talking to you!"

"I don't know, Mother. What are you thinking?" Rebekah was as surprised by her snarkiness as everyone else.

"Hey! That's not an acceptable way to speak to your mother, Rebekah," her usually very quiet father reprimanded her.

"I know. I'm sorry, Mother." She refused to make eye contact with either of them. From the corner of her eye, she could see that Pammy was understandably very uncomfortable. Her friend, head down, played with her food. This was something new to all of them. Rebekah had never been rude to her parents.

"Mother? Why are you calling me Mother?"

"I've decided that it suits you," Rebekah answered, quite matter-of-factly.

"I don't care for it at all. It sounds rather cold," she whispered.

"It suits you." Rebekah shrugged her shoulders. She then stood, motioned to Pammy, walked out of the kitchen, and continued right out the cottage door. But not before grabbing a handful of bacon, which her mother always cooked to the perfect crispness she so loved, and two warm-from-the-oven honey buns.

"19th Nervous Breakdown"

"What was that?" Pammy said in the loudest whisper Rebekah had ever heard.

"I'm not sure. I need to think. I might be having a nervous breakdown or something," Rebekah reasoned. She had read about such a thing in the *Reader's Digest* once. At the time, she just knew that nothing like that would ever happen to her but was fascinated by the story, nonetheless.

In fact, Rebekah loved every story in the *Reader's Digest* magazines. She hated that she read the whole thing in a day or two and had to wait another month for the next one. She read every article, every joke, and every feature story. She even did the Word Power game. Her father let her circle her answers in the magazine. Even though he liked to do the puzzle too, he didn't need to circle the answers, he memorized them. It was the same with the newspaper puzzles. He did the crossword and the crypto quote—all of them in his head before going to work, and he let her mother fill them out herself. He was brilliant that way. Playing cards with him, from what Rebekah was told, was a lesson in humility. He remembered every card that had been played and was, therefore, able to figure out what every other player was holding. As soon as she outgrew Go Fish and War, she decided that the days of playing cards with him were over. Once she realized that he had been letting her win, she just didn't see the point of learning how to lose to him.

"What are we going to do?" Pammy asked.

"Right now, let's just go get some ice cream."

"I don't think you're having a nervous breakdown, Rebekah. I don't really know what a nervous breakdown is, but it sounds bad, and I'm pretty sure if you were, you wouldn't even want ice cream. So, I think we're going to be okay," Pammy encouraged her.

"Well, whatever this is, I'm not going to let it ruin this vacation. Mother and Father will just have to wait. I cannot be thinking about their problems right now," Rebekah decided.

"Do you think they will wait?"

"They will have no choice. We will do what we have to do."

Pammy didn't ask her what she meant, which was probably for the best.

And with that, while handing a honey bun to her friend, Rebekah took her first bite of the now-cold pastry. Finding it quite delicious, she decided to finish the rest with the ice cream that awaited them. Pammy followed suit, and the two of them merrily made their way to the Dairy Queen, happily noticing for the first time that the rain had finally ended.

Unfortunately, the lull did not last. The rain started up again, heavier than before, while the girls made their way to the pavilion with their treats. A joint decision was made to return to the cottage. The day had the makings of a complete wash-out.

While running back to the cottage, Rebekah gave serious thought to how she would approach her parents. She had hoped to have more time to think about it.

She grabbed Pammy's arm and stopped abruptly, practically causing her friend to fall backward.

"I may just be a genius, Pammy. Listen to this. Since I'm not quite prepared to deal with my parents, I'll tell them that I cannot discuss anything about what just happened because I need time to process some newly acquired information. I will explain to them that this newfound knowledge has caused me much angst. Isn't that a great word—*angst*? They will be so impressed by my maturity that they will have to respect my wishes. Come on, let's get back quick before I forget what I want to say." Rebekah took a deep breath and grabbed Pammy's hand to get out of the rain.

"Your car is gone." Pammy announced as they approached the cottage. "And look, our floats are propped up against the porch."

Hmm? Why would the car be gone? In all the years they had been coming to the beach, Rebekah couldn't remember one time when her parents left in the car without her. As for the floats, she was pleased to see that while Greg and David might not have bothered to ask to use them, they obviously had the good manners to bring them back.

The lingering scent of bacon filled each room as the girls made their way through the cottage checking to see if either parent was still there. The last room they checked, the kitchen, was empty as well. The breakfast dishes sat exactly where they were when Rebekah had rushed out. Her mother always cleaned everything before leaving the kitchen—well, almost always—remembering the hazy memory from earlier.

Rebekah waited all day for them to return. She rehearsed her speech over and over. She had to get it just right so as to leave them with no choice but to let it go—for now. But they didn't come home until dinnertime, and it was clear that they had rehearsed their own little speech.

"Where were you?" Rebekah barked before her parents had gotten through the front door.

"That's not important," her mother stated.

Her father held up a hand. "It's been a very long day, and we all have things on our minds. So, let's just call it a night. You girls can fix yourselves something to eat. There's plenty of sandwich stuff to choose from. Your mother and I will be in our room watching TV for the evening. Goodnight."

Rebekah was keenly aware that Pammy had already discreetly made her way to the bedroom and had quietly closed the door. Rebekah's parents did the same, albeit not so discreetly and not particularly quietly.

What was that?? I didn't even get to explain my angst!

"Pammy," Rebekah called out. "What do you want to eat?"

Pammy opened the bedroom door, poked her head and looked around. Rebekah waved for her to come with her to the kitchen.

They did not speak about any of the night's strangeness. They ate. Pammy suggested that they clean the kitchen and Rebekah agreed. It would be an example to her parents of her maturity level. Since she didn't get the chance to tell them yet, she would at least show them.

Once every plate, coffee cup, fork, knife and spoon were washed, dried and put away and the table had been wiped off, the two of them made their way to the bedroom, got ready, listened to some music, and called it a night.

🙞 🙜

Tuesday, July 12, 1966

"Boys"

The girls awoke to a bright sun illuminating the entire bedroom.

"Oh, my gosh. Please tell me this sunshine is going to last today," Rebekah said to no one in particular. With day four now ahead of them, she set her sights on the here and now. It would be best to simply forget yesterday completely and focus on the important things—the boys.

&ं&

"Raindrops"

The four of them had been sitting in their usual spot for what seemed like an hour or more, what with everything the girls—mostly Rebekah—had to tell them. It only seemed fair to keep them in the loop since they too were witnesses to the infamous "pier sightings."

Rebekah finished telling her story and blew out a breath.

Johnny glanced at Pammy, then back at her. "Um . . . what's upset you so bad?"

"Why am I so upset? Did you really just ask me that?" Rebekah couldn't believe he didn't get it.

"I'm just trying to understand, is all," he replied.

"What's there to understand?" Rebekah's voice was considerably raised at this point.

Pammy and Hank, who had been half listening, rose at the same time and crept away down the beach.

Johnny sat quietly until they'd gone some distance away. He turned to Rebekah and stared at her for a few seconds.

"You have the most beautiful blue eyes I think I've ever seen."

Although at a total loss for words, her mind was reeling — again.

Are you for real? I just yelled at you for no good reason, and you decide this is the time to woo me? I like that word "woo." Old fashioned with a nice ring to it.

"I've been wanting to tell you that since that first day. But, well, it didn't seem like the right time. This did, is all." He shrugged.

Rebekah's angered expression softened. Her shoulders relaxed and, even if she had wanted to, she would not have been able to hold back her smile. But she still wanted—needed—to talk this situation out. Why she felt the desire to do so with Johnny, she didn't quite understand. She'd just add that to the growing list of "Things That Are Not Understood by Rebekah." Maybe because he wasn't a part of it all. He didn't even know her parents, had never met them. He had no reason to side with them.

She turned to look at him and briefly contemplated returning the beautiful eyes compliment, but decided against it. For the time being anyway. "Can I ask you something?"

"Of course."

She took a deep breath and exhaled slowly. "What is it that you don't understand?"

He cocked his head and scratched his chin. "Well, you are really worked up over something that you don't even know what it is you're worked up over, is all. I mean that in the least judgy way imaginable," he rushed to add.

Rebekah smiled at his use of such diplomacy—ah, another great word.

"How old are you?" she asked, contemplating his last perfect response.

"Why?" He grinned. "You afraid I'm too young for ya?" He winked, which caused Rebekah's whole body to warm from within, and heat rushed to her cheeks.

Without thinking about it, she just went with her feelings—Pammy was right after all—why play games or keep them guessing?

"I've never been kissed," she informed him. Emboldened by the no-more-games decision, she pressed on. "Would you like to be my first?"

Johnny leaned toward her, gently cupped his hand under her chin, eased her face toward his and placed the softest, sweetest, and shortest kiss on her welcoming lips—a kiss that was so much softer, sweeter, shorter, and better than any she had imagined. And she had certainly been imagining many of late. She poised herself to receive another. Since a second didn't come, she pulled back and shifted her gaze to the ocean, wiggling her toes deep into the sand. To think that she'd just assumed that her first kiss would be with Mark. Mark—she hadn't thought of him at all for a couple of days.

"Seventeen. You?" Johnny spoke first after a period of silence.

"How old do you think I am?" she responded, allowing him to ponder another perfect answer.

"Well, never been kissed, hmm?" he mused. "Sixteen?"

"Too young or too old?" Rebekah didn't correct his guess.

"Let me think . . . I'll get back to you on that," he countered—and then, ever so teasingly—flashed that beautiful smile of his.

The warmth, the butterflies, the flush, all rushed in and over her with such intensity, she had to turn away. Who knew what she might do if she didn't get herself together.

Is this what love feels like?

Pammy and Hank came back into view. Rebekah shot up and brushed the sand off. "I'm going to the pavilion." She needed to clear her head, and music was always the best way to do it.

She had never experienced such contrasting emotions before. It had her so churned up inside, she ran ahead of the others so as not to expose her tears. Sad tears, happy tears, confusing tears—like raindrops falling from her eyes.

"Emotions"

Johnny caught up with her just before she got to the pavilion. Lightly touching her arm, he teasingly asked, "Something I said, or am I just a really bad kisser?"

"Neither," Rebekah assured him, knowing full well he did not need to be assured. She met his gaze. "I'm a great big ball of emotions, and Johnny, you are the reason behind all of the good ones."

Maintaining the face-to-face stance and biting her lip a bit, she added, "I shall call you Johnny Bean."

"You shall call me what?"

"Johnny Bean," she repeated. "Like Jelly Bean."

"Girl, I got no idea what the heck you are talking about." Johnny raised his eyebrows—clearly puzzled but not seeming at all upset.

"Because you are so sweet. Also, I give all my favorite people nicknames."

Johnny chuckled, took her hand, led her up the three steps and straight onto the dance floor. "Emotions" had just started playing. How fitting. They danced closely and slowly, neither one singing along.

By the time Brenda Lee finished, Pammy and Hank had made their way to a corner table where Hank had already purchased and placed four small soda bottles.

Johnny had finished half of his in one gulp before Rebekah took her first sip. As she did, tears welled up in the corner of her eyes—eyes that had been locked with Johnny's since they sat down. And all she could think was how unfair the whole thing was.

"Pammy," she said, eyes still locked into his. "Do you need to go to the bathroom?" The girls had devised this plan years ago when one or the other had something very important to say—in private.

"Not really," Pammy answered. Since she and Hank were whispering to each other, it was clear to Rebekah that Pammy just didn't hear her.

"Ahem, Pammy, I thought you told me you needed to go to the bathroom."

"When did I say that?" Pammy went from oblivious to aware in one breath. "Oh, yes, yes, I did say that. I do need to go. Yes, yes, I do need to," she started just bumbling.

Rebekah saved her from herself by grabbing her hand and leading her toward the bathroom. "What is the matter with you, Pamela Rose?"

"Geez, you sound like my mother when she's mad at me. You are not my mother, so do not act like you are. Please."

"Sorry, weird things are coming over me. But you totally forgot our plan. And I really need to talk to you. I'm in love. And I wanted you to be the first one to know."

"Uh, shouldn't the boy you're in love with be the first to know? But since you did tell me first, who is it—Johnny or Mark?"

"What?"

Pammy laughed. "I'm totally messing with you. Of course, I know it's Mark. Just kidding! But seriously, how can you be in love with a boy you just met like two seconds ago? A boy whose last name you don't even know." She paused and glared at Rebekah.

Rebekah did not correct her assumption. She was right.

"What if it's some horrible name like vomit—Johnny Vomit?"

"Pammy! I am being totally serious, and you're just making fun of me."

Pammy scrunched up her face and reached out to place a hand on Rebekah's arm. "I'm so sorry. I really am. But I do think you should at least find out his last name, and maybe his age, and maybe where he lives—for starters."

"Seventeen. He thinks I'm sixteen."

"Why does he think you're sixteen?" Pammy asked.

"Well, that's kinda what I let him think," Rebekah confessed.

Pammy put her hands on her hips. "You do know that you turned fifteen less than a month ago."

"It just happened really fast. I couldn't stop it," Rebekah said, trying to excuse it. She knew that Pammy would call it another lie of omission. Maybe she was right.

Rebekah skipped over that to get to the most important point. The point that she just had to get out of her mind. The epiphany—how many amazing words was that in just one day?—she had sitting across from Johnny not five minutes ago.

"Pammy, this is all so unfair. I've heard it said that life can be so cruel sometimes, and now I totally get it. Life is totally cruel." Rebekah's eyes threatened to fill with tears.

Pammy didn't reply, but Rebekah recognized the look. She was worried about Rebekah. Worried about her falling in love so fast or being what she'd call overdramatic, Rebekah couldn't tell.

"Why did I have to meet the boy I want to spend the rest of my life with now? Why? I'm not even as old as he thinks I am, and he's only seventeen, and I'll never see him again, and our week is almost over, and I am going to be miserable and lonely and broken-hearted the rest of my life because it's almost over before it's even begun and—"

"Rebekah, slow down; catch your breath. Let's take a deep breath and go back out there before they decide to leave. They're gonna think we have abandoned them. We can think about everything and talk about it later. Right now, two super cute boys are waiting for us to come back. Two super cute boys who want to be with us."

"Oh, my gosh, Pammy, you're right. Let's go. I will try to make the best of my worst day ever."

Pammy shook her head.

Wednesday, July 13, 1966

༄༅

"All Alone Am I"

Rebekah had been awake since four after a night of tossing and turning.

The dreaded encounter with her parents, especially her mother, was bound to happen sooner than later, and last night was it. But the heated argument with raised voices that she had expected did not happen. Not the one she prepared herself for, rehearsed for. The elaborate speech she memorized to explain in detail—her angst—and finally have her say.

But she didn't have her say. Not in the least. The evening did not once get heated; in fact, calm and polite conversation prevailed. And much to Rebekah's disappointment, none of her concerns were even addressed. Her parents just played the parent card and called it a done deal. What was that about? *They must have a ton more to hide than I suspected.*

They knew they had the upper hand, the parent hand, which they played by refusing to answer a single one of her questions. And she would give that to them . . . for the time being.

Thus, the tossing and turning—and the ridiculous early rising.

With her trusted diary and favorite pen—that week's favorite—in hand, she quietly made her way out the bedroom and the house without being detected. She would surely be able to sort everything out by doing what she always did whenever she just couldn't do so any other way. She would think and write and think and write and think some more. And write some more.

The quiet, the beauty of the pristine beach, the beginning signs of daylight, each brought comfort in its own way. The quiet—ah, no words needed, for they would just bring noise. The clean, uncluttered sand that offered no proof of human life except that evidenced by her footprints alone. The sun, peeking from the horizon, promised that a beautiful summer day awaited her. It was all just for her. Sitting at the top of the wide strand, she started to write. But not at all what she'd gone there to write.

The page began to fill with her immense appreciation of all that surrounded her. The peace that came over her as the light breeze gently blew through her uncombed hair. Of this and more, she wrote. Not about the issues and the angst, but about the possibility that something or someone much bigger and stronger and more knowledgeable—than she, her parents, or anyone else she knew—might exist. Though it seemed quite unlikely, she left it at that, her diary entry for the day was complete. And she certainly did not understand any more than she did before she awoke early that morning. But she felt different, a bit better. Yet another mystery to be solved at another time. The mystery of a higher power to be considered on another day.

Later that day, she and Pammy would make the best of one of their last days in paradise. She simply could not, would not, allow all the occurrences, thoughts, and contemplations get in the way of what was most important. It was as simple as that. She would eventually have her say and get to the bottom of her mother's secret life and her father's too, if he had one. But she needed to prioritize her goals and all the rest could—must—wait. Her focus was on that which was most important: her happiness and her love life. So be it!

"Bye Bye Baby"

"I was starting to think you ran away," Pammy told Rebekah, as they made their way back to their spot.

"Well, you were asleep when I came to bed. Trust me, I totally would have awakened you if there had been anything to report. I don't know much of anything for sure, but what I do know is that something is definitely going on. My parents are not talking to me about it, so I'm on my own to figure it out. Plus, I didn't want to wake you so early this morning. That, and I just needed to get down here early by myself to try to figure some stuff out."

"So, what did you figure out?" Pammy asked the obvious question.

"Nothing, really. But I've got some ideas," Rebekah told Pammy, knowing that was not at all true. She just wanted to leave it at that without mentioning all that she had written about. She didn't even mention having a diary. After all, the whole point of a diary was to record one's own private thoughts. Since the thoughts were unknown to anyone, shouldn't the place where they were recorded be unknown as well?

"I'm going to take your advice, Pammy," Rebekah said, changing the subject.

"My advice? When did I give you advice?" They both knew that Pammy was not the advice-giver in their friendship.

"I'm going to find out Johnny's last name. And I'm going to tell him mine."

"Ah." Pammy grinned.

"And then I'm going to tell him that I love him. And I just know that he'll tell me the same. And don't try to talk me out of it. You're the one who is always saying that pretending is the same as lying. And I am telling you, right here and right now that I have seen the light. I realize that you have been right all along."

Pammy stepped in front of her, causing Rebekah to bump right into her. Pammy looked squarely in her eyes and with a firm voice said, "Since when have you ever listened to me about romance? What the heck would I know about it? Rebekah, of all the times I've ever said anything to you, it was never about anything this serious. But since you suddenly seem convinced that I have something to offer, let me offer this: You are going to scare the poor guy away, and you will never see him again!"

Rebekah pushed Pammy aside and continued the few feet to their spot in silence. After carefully placing her beach towel on the sand and pulling the transistor out of the bag, she sat, staring ahead at the white-capped waves rushing to the shore, wishing that was all she ever had to do. Just sit and watch the beautiful, powerful ocean ebb and flow.

"Well, Pammy, I look at it this way," she finally spoke. "I'm never going to see him again whether I tell him I love him or whether I don't. And since I'm not ever going to see him again, I want him at least to know that I do. That and my last name—I want him to know my last name—in case he wants to look me up some day." End of discussion.

In silent agreement to just live in the moment, they slathered themselves with oil for some much-desired tanning. Rebekah tapped the transistor radio dial, finding the station they loved. She began singing along with Chris Montez, who was halfway through "Call Me."

As soon as it ended, before the next one started, she added, "And my phone number. He needs my phone number."

They both fell asleep as The Supremes and Rebekah finished, "Back in My Arms Again." Rebekah did pose one concern before dozing off, "I wonder where the guys are. I want to spend the whole rest of the day with Johnny Bean."

By the time they woke up, lunchtime had come and gone. A walk to the Dairy Queen was certainly in order. But Rebekah didn't want to leave their spot. Johnny would be there any minute. Pammy agreed that just one of them should make the trek up and back. But there was no guarantee that the ice cream would survive the short trip. It was worth the chance, so off she went, leaving Rebekah to her thoughts again.

Where are you, Johnny Bean? I bet you don't like your nickname and changed your mind about being with me. No, you met another girl between last night and this morning? You somehow figured out that I am not really sixteen? You decided you just want to spend the rest of your beach vacation hanging out with your friends? You never even liked me and decided to stop leading me on, that's it, isn't it?

"Hurry up and eat this while there's still time," Pammy interrupted her thoughts, thrusting a butterscotch-dipped ice cream cone in her face. It was all Rebekah could do to lick all the melting sweetness before she ended up wearing it. As they made their way to the water to give their sticky hands a salt bath, Rebekah thought she caught a glimpse of Hank walking toward them. But where was Johnny?

It was not Hank, but rather a boy they had never seen before, approaching as if he knew them.

"Are you Pammy and Rachel?" he asked, looking back and forth at each of them.

"I'm Pammy. But there's no Rachel," Pammy informed him.

He studied Rebekah. "Oh, well what's your name then?"

"Who are you and how do you know who we are?" asked Rebekah, without giving him her name.

"Hank wanted me to find you and tell you something," he said, with no introduction. "He said to look for the two cutest girls on the beach."

"Why didn't Hank come?" asked Pammy.

"He didn't want to leave Johnny alone," he responded. "Johnny just found out this morning that his twin brother was killed in Viet Nam. We are all heading home as soon as I get back."

The girls stood there, dumbfounded . . . shocked . . . speechless.

"I'm Hank's brother, Tommy," he turned and started running away.

"Wait, Tommy," called Rebekah. "Where is home?"

"Philadelphia," he yelled back and was gone before they could ask anything else. There was so much more Rebekah wanted to ask. But the boy was now lost in the crowd. Johnny was leaving, and she still didn't know his last name.

Life is getting more unfair by the minute.

"We Gotta Get Out of This Place"

Rebekah was in no mood to talk about it. Or anything else for that matter. The two unsuspecting boys who approached them as they sat quietly watching the foamy water rush over their toes before slinking back out to sea, were simply in the wrong place at the wrong time.

Rebekah not only failed to return a cheesy grin, but she also shot a look that said all they needed to not hear. They stepped back, wide-eyed, and took off like they had encountered a man-eating shark. Maybe they had.

Focusing attention back to the lapping waves, tears falling onto her red, freckled cheeks, she mumbled, "There goes my life, Pammy. Just washing away like the tide. I so wish we had never come here this year. Why do my parents come here anyway? There's plenty of great beaches in North Carolina."

Pammy remained silent.

"He lied to me," Rebekah stated, with no hint of emotion. "Johnny Bean lied to me."

"When?"

"When he told me he's seventeen, that's when," her voice still flat.

"How do you know that's a lie?"

"Well, first of all, he didn't even tell me had a twin brother, never mind that. If they were seventeen, his twin wouldn't have been in Viet Nam. I don't know much about the war and all, but I do know he would have to be eighteen—at least."

"Oh, wow."

Suddenly, Rebekah jumped up. "Let's go, Pammy." She made a beeline away from the beach.

"What?" Pammy shot up. "Where are we going?"

Rebekah glanced back without slowing down. Pammy was stuffing the towels and radio into the bags that were almost left behind.

"Philadelphia, Pammy. We are going to Philadelphia."

ॐ

"Ticket to Ride"

Rebekah did not share her plan with Pammy, and Pammy did not ask although her friend studied her with pursed lips as they hosed the sand off themselves.

"Girls, I'm so glad you're back." Rebekah's mother waved them into the kitchen as soon as the screen door slammed behind them. "Your dad's grilling burgers, and I made coleslaw with carrots, and the baked beans have brown sugar and bacon. I also made your grandma's chocolate cake with peanut butter frosting—all your favorites, sweetheart."

Rebekah's suspicions about the over-the-top, everything-is-grand act outweighed her desire to tend to her gnawing belly and led her to snarkily reply, "We're not hungry, Mother."

Pammy fell into the seat of the closest kitchen chair. Right. All they'd eaten since their skimpy breakfast was an ice cream cone.

Rebekah's mother had turned away to rescue the almost-overcooked beans from the oven, and her father hadn't quite gotten through the back door with the platter of his specialty burgers screaming with savory aroma, making Rebekah the only witness to Pammy's close call.

As she shoved a glass of water into her friend's hand, Rebekah gave her a look that said drink all of this—now. As she did so, she realized that this was the perfect time to kill two birds with one stone. *Who said that anyway? Was it Benjamin Franklin? Or was it Mark Twain?*

They would enjoy the much-needed sustenance and then, since everyone was present, she would spill the beans, so to speak.

"Okay, Mother. We'll go ahead and eat a little since you went to so much trouble."

"Don't be silly. This was no trouble at all. I always love it when we all eat together." Her mother seemed almost giddy.

The parents offered pleasantries while the girls scarfed down their meals in silence. Rebekah hoped that her parents didn't notice Pammy's shaking hands. Her mother would go into nurse mode, and the plan would be canceled before she even had a chance to present it.

As anxious as she was to get on with her plan, she had to wait. There was no way she was going to miss out on Grandma's All Occasion Cake. That cake had won its fair share of Blue Ribbons at the North Carolina State Fair for a reason. A slice of perfection. Perfect end to a perfect meal.

Stomachs full . . . the time was right. A slight tap on Pammy's leg was all she offered to warn her of what was to come.

"Do we need to go to the bathroom?" Pammy asked.

"No." Rebekah looked at her parents who were starting to clean up and raised her voice to get the attention that the announcement required. "No, we do not need to go to the bathroom, but I do have some very important plans to share with both of you, Mother and Father."

"My goodness, this sounds ominous," said her father as he continued to clear the table.

"I need you to stop what you're doing and listen," she insisted. "This is very important."

"Should I leave?" asked Pammy, nodding, probably hoping Rebekah would say yes.

Rebekah ignored her question.

"Pammy and I have decided that as soon as we get home, we are going to go to Philadelphia."

"You most certainly are not," her mother exclaimed, continuing to clean up.

"Don't be ridiculous, young lady," her father answered in a—to Rebekah's mind—very superior way.

"Father, please do not patronize me," she responded, so that he would know that she knew what that was.

That got both parents' attention.

"Rebekah, what has gotten into you? First, calling us Mother and Father, and now speaking to your father as if he is . . . well . . . as if he is not your father."

Her father met her gaze. "This is absurd, we are not discussing this further. End of discussion."

"Mother, I'm not sure that Father knows some of the things that I have learned on this vacation," Rebekah snipped, glaring at her mother with narrowed eyes.

"What is that supposed to mean, young lady?" his voice rose.

"Why don't you ask Mother," Rebekah replied, keeping her voice calm.

Her father looked at her mother with the unspoken question written all over his face.

After several minutes of silently staring at Rebekah, her mother spoke up.

"I cannot and will not sit here and be humiliated by my own daughter. And in front of Pammy, no less. What must your parents think of us?" She was upset but not crying. Her face was flushed, and it seemed to Rebekah that she was holding back tears. Her hands rested on the table, and she began to pick at her cuticles.

Rebekah didn't give Pammy a chance to respond. "Pammy and I will be taking a bus. I have enough money saved up from birthdays and Christmases to cover both fares. You probably have some money too, don't you, Pammy?" She didn't wait for an answer. "We will leave very soon after we get home. Probably the next day or maybe the day after that. Either way, we are leaving right away. Pammy's parents will think she is staying another week at our house."

"Listen, Rebekah, you are a fifteen-year-old girl, and you and Pammy are not getting on a bus and going anywhere alone," insisted her father. "What's in Philadelphia anyway? Besides, you do realize all I'd have to do is call the police, right?"

"You could. But they would question me. And I would have to tell them everything I know. And I'm just not sure, Father, whether you even know everything I know. Mother, does he?"

"Rebekah, you only think you know something. I have no idea what you are talking about, but let's go into the bedroom together, and you can talk to me about it," her mother suggested.

"Mother, I know that I saw you on the pier the other day." The moment of truth. She was about to find out if, indeed, that was her mother smoking cigarettes and hugging a strange man.

Rebekah was more convinced than ever that her mother was hiding something when she jumped up from the table, ran out, and slammed the back door behind her. By the look on her father's face, it was clear that he was completely in the dark—just as she had suspected.

It was brilliant. Everything was going to work out perfectly. She would be seeing Johnny soon. All she and Pammy had to do now was figure out all the little details. That shouldn't be too difficult.

꧁꧂

Part 1: Summer 1966

This Diary Belongs To:

Rebekah Louise Lang

PRIVATE*****************KEEP OUT**

ENTRY DATE: Tuesday, July 12, 1966

First time I've ever been on the beach this early. It's so beautiful. It's perfect. How strange to be the only one here, not another person in sight. The way the sun is just beginning to appear. And the ocean is mesmerizing—mesmerizing, great word! Imagine if the world was flat. It sure looks that way. Like the ocean stops, and everything just falls right off. I've never thought too much about it before, but how could something this beautiful just magically appear out of nowhere? Unless there really is a God who really did create everything. I mean, the breeze in my hair is light and warm. I feel it. I can't see it, but I know it exists. Lots of stuff exists that we can't see, right? Maybe God too! If so, he must be way smarter than any grown-up I know. Oh, well, maybe I'll think about all of that later, I need to get ready to see Johnny. My love life awaits!

ENTRY DATE: Monday, July 18, 1966

SO much has happened since we've been home. I can't believe the entry above was my only one while we were at the beach. I think I might have been too upset to even put everything into words. Which, for the record, has never happened to me before!!

First of all, ever since I actually confronted my parents about seeing my mother on the pier, they have been kinda ignoring me. Which I think is really weird. I don't know why they don't just tell me what's going on. But what's even weirder is that they said for me to go ahead and go to Philadelphia if that's what I want to do. WHAT?? Anyway, Pammy had a receipt with Hank's address on it but guess what?? We couldn't even read it. His writing is atrocious (great word). We think the city is D E R D Y or something like that. We are going to the library today to find a newspaper or look on one of those machine things to see if we can find an obituary notice for Johnny's brother, even though we don't know his last name. But I figure since he died in war and he's pretty young, we should be able to find it.

ENTRY DATE: Friday, July 22, 1966

I am devastated!! I am destroyed!! Everything I worked so hard for is OVER!! I couldn't even write anything until now. I can hardly see what I'm writing. I have never cried this hard in my whole life. I bet I didn't even cry like this when I was a baby—and my parents have always told me I cried all the time. I must have been practicing for this day! Well, the city turned out to be Darby, not Derdy. It's like a part of Philadelphia. But we couldn't find anything about a soldier's funeral. My parents were even going to pay for us to stay in a hotel!! My dad knows somebody who knows somebody that was going to make it happen. They probably told me all that because they somehow knew it wasn't gonna work out anyway. I don't know when I will ever be able to write in this diary again. I just want to die! I'm going to stay in my bedroom the rest of the summer and listen to music all by myself. Nobody will even be allowed in here. Except for Pammy. She can come in. She's devastated too— I think!

ENTRY DATE: Tuesday, September 6, 1966

First Day of School. I saw Mark. We didn't have time to talk much, but he acts like he still likes me. A girl can tell. He is really nice. I wouldn't tell anybody but Pammy and you that I do like him, but I still REALLY like Johnny Bean. I am glad that Mark still likes me. I doubt that Johnny does. He probably doesn't even remember me. What difference does it make? We will never see each other again. I don't know how much I will be writing for a while. My life is so boring that I don't have anything to say. Except: I am still going to figure out everything I can about what was going on with my mother—I started calling them Mamma and Daddy again. Oh, and I already got two books from the school library . . . "Gone with the Wind" and "To Kill a Mockingbird." They are both books about problems with coloreds and white people and stuff; I've been wanting to understand more.

ENTRY DATE: Christmas Day 1966

This was a really great Christmas! Mark got me a beautiful cameo ring!! I got him The Beatles "Revolver" album. The songs are SO GOOD!! My favorite is "Eleanor Rigby," and he said his is "Yellow Submarine." I love The Beatles SO MUCH!! They are the BEST band to ever exist!! My parents got me some clothes and my favorite hose and some hot curlers and lots of stocking stuffers. Other stuff too, I can't remember it all. Oh, yeah, a new diary too. And some underwear and pj's.

ENTRY DATE: Wednesday, February 15, 1967

I can't believe that I haven't written anything in here since Christmas. Yesterday was Valentine's Day, and we had a dance at school. Mama bought me a really pretty dress and even let me get my hair done at a salon. That was amazing. Pammy and I rode together since my parents don't want me to date until I'm sixteen. But Mark and I danced. We did the twist and the pony and the mashed potato. We didn't do any slow dancing, but we spent most of the night together. He is sweet. He asked me to go steady. I told him yes. I just think we might as well be going steady now. But I will only tell you and Pammy this: I did think about Johnny some, and it made me really sad. Mark asked me what was wrong, and I told him I was feeling emotional about going steady. I didn't tell Pammy that part, she would say it was lying—but it's not the same because I said it so I wouldn't hurt his feelings, which is very kind of me, I think. Plus, he might have asked for the ring back, and I love it so much.

ENTRY DATE: Tuesday, May 16, 1967

Doing homework and looking for a notebook and found this under some books. What in the world have I been doing since Valentine's Day?? Nothing worth writing about obviously! Mark and I are still going steady. School will be over in a couple of weeks, and I will be a junior next year!! I can't believe it. And I will finally be sixteen at the end of June. YAY!!! All my friends are already sixteen. Pammy's been sixteen since October!!

ENTRY DATE: Monday, May 29, 1967

Another school year almost behind me. Pammy and I are going to an end-of-school party on Saturday night at Sheila's house. I'm really excited. Mark won't be there because his family is going to the lake. It will be fun to hang out with just girls. I finally finished both the books that I got a long time ago. I had to keep renewing "Gone with the Wind." I can't say that I understand anything more than I ever did. I cried when I read "To Kill and Mockingbird." I don't think I want to be able to say that

I understand. I think it is just awful. I've been thinking about the day that Johnny took us to that fence. I cried a bit thinking about him too. I haven't been able to forget him yet. Why can't I just forget about him??

ENTRY DATE: Friday, June 23, 1967

My parents told me today that we are going back to the beach cottage! I called Pammy and told her. We talked for a long time about last summer. Even so, we still can't wait!! If something sad or bad has to happen, it might as well be at the beach, right??

Part 2: Summer 1967

Saturday, July 8, 1967

"Different Drum"

"Strange how things look the same, huh?" Rebekah stopped to breathe in the beachiness. "Even though nothing really is. At least the beach always smells the same."

Pammy was the first to say what they had both been thinking since they left home, "Being here really does bring it all right back, huh?"

"I wasn't sure we would come back this summer, but here we are. Pammy, we have to do everything we can to make the best of this week. We cannot waste even one minute not having fun." Rebekah sighed. *I just can't let myself think of Johnny the whole time.*

Making their way across the familiar crunchy surface, Rebekah stopped again, but not to fill her nostrils. Someone else had taken their spot. No one had ever been in their perfect spot before.

"Well, like I just said, nothing is the same anymore." Figuring there was no point in pouting about it, Rebekah found a new perfect spot. It was actually more perfect. How had she not realized it before? Pammy followed her up to the top of the strand where a sand dune separated the beach from the brownish-green lawn of the one-story cottage sitting several yards back. The same spot where Rebekah sat last summer to write the only diary entry of the whole week last summer. The memory prompted her to question out loud. "Hmm, did I remember my diary?"

"You keep a diary?" Pammy asked.

"Sure, don't you?" Rebekah had not meant to let that information out of the bag.

"I don't. But if I did, I would have already told you. How long have you had a diary?" Pammy crossed her arms.

"You're acting like you do when you say I lied about something. Only worse," Rebekah shot back at her.

"Well, it kinda feels the same. And it feels personal. I tell you everything. I tell you how I feel about everything. I thought we both did. You obviously have someone else to tell everything to. Your new best friend. I bet you even nicknamed her Di or something."

Rebekah spread both beach blankets in front of the dune, calmy pulled the radio out, and lay on her stomach with her legs bent at the knees and feet to the cloudless sky above. Finding her favorite radio station was easier than usual.

"I can't talk to you when you're like this, Pammy."

Rebekah started singing along to "Different Drum." As soon as musical notes took over the words she continued, "And for the record I don't remember you ever being like this before. Not like this. I don't know why it's such a big deal that I have a diary, and you don't. Maybe we travel to the beat of a different drum sometimes, huh?"

"Oh, my gosh, Rebekah. Everything in life is not a stupid song."

Rebekah didn't answer, but she absolutely disagreed with that statement. For two reasons. Everything in life was, by all means, a song, and just as important; there were no stupid songs.

For the next fifteen minutes the only sound that came from either of them was Rebekah singing along with every tune that blasted from the small device.

Pammy finally spoke up. "I'm sorry. My period started yesterday.

For some reason, everything about this one is like ten times worse than ever before."

Rebekah sat up, "Ah geez, Pammy. That really stinks. I guess I'm sorry too. If you really want to, you can read my diary. I promise, I never write anything in there that I haven't already told you." *I'm pretty sure.*

"That's okay. I think we all have things that we don't tell anyone about," Pammy assured her. "Things that we just keep to ourselves."

Rebekah ignored Pammy's furrowed brows. "I'm going to get my feet wet."

She needed a little alone time. She was starting to think about Johnny again, and she was determined not to talk about it. Maybe if she didn't talk about him, she would stop thinking about him. Maybe if she stopped thinking about him, she wouldn't talk about him. Maybe she could have the fun time she was determined to have. Problem was, she was surrounded by everything that reminded her of him.

I am only sixteen years old, and I will not obsess over a guy I knew for five days and will never see again. This is ridiculous! There is something seriously wrong with me.

Swooshing the water around with her feet while deep in thought, it hit her. To get Johnny out of her mind, she would focus on something of—almost—the same level of importance. That week was the quintessential—ah such a great word—opportunity to readdress the whole secret lives of her mother and father. Every time she'd tried to bring it up after they got home last summer, they'd change the subject or leave the room. Finally, she'd given up. But . . .

This is where it started, and this is where it shall end.

☙ ❧

"Silence Is Golden"

Getting ready for the pavilion just wasn't the same as it used to be. Even before Johnny, Rebekah always got really excited and took way more time selecting her outfit and putting on makeup than she ever did at home. She always took extra time helping Pammy pick out just the right outfit. Two super cool girls were bound to get way more attention than one—any day.

But not that night. A pair of pale green shorts and her favorite Myrtle Beach T-shirt was just fine. She even wore her white Keds, something she would never have done before. Not to the pavilion where meeting boys was almost as important as the music—almost. That night, whatever Pammy wore made no difference to her. Who cared? All that mattered was that the music would be blasting. On that, she could be sure. She clung to anything and everything she could depend on those days. Like Mark. She could always depend on him. And Pammy, of course.

"Girls, I want you to be sure to eat something before you go. We don't want a repeat of last summer," Rebekah's mother called from the kitchen.

I cannot even believe that she bought up last summer. I know she's talking about Pammy feeling sick, but she just opened the door for me to walk right in. We most definitely will be taking the time to eat. And time to talk about a few other things from last summer.

Rebekah stood motionless staring at the red and white Formica tabletop, oblivious to the many other changes surrounding her. To get her wits about her, she moved slowly to the closest of the four matching vinyl chairs and perused the kitchen.

"Who did all this?" she asked, trying but not succeeding, to sound nonchalant.

"We did," her father proclaimed.

"And the owners just let you come in and change everything? Everything that had been the way it was—like forever?" No effort at nonchalance this time.

"The owners were thrilled," her mother exclaimed, as if she thought Rebekah should be thrilled as well.

Why are they both acting like I was privy (great word) to all of this?

"We . . . Are . . . The . . . Owners," they cheered in unison, and Rebekah wondered where the pom-poms were for their little, well-rehearsed, routine.

"So, is this a thing now? Are you just gonna spring new stuff on me every time we come here? Since when is this *our* cottage? Has it always been . . . you just forgot to mention it before? Or did you just buy it, so you could get rid of that table with the deep scratch in it?"

Ear-splitting silence filled the kitchen.

"All Alone Am I"

When Rebekah left, she knew not to look for Pammy, who'd disappeared before making it to the kitchen. Rebekah's head spun. Her knees shook. Her heart was racing. And her thoughts were all over the place. Getting away from her parents was all that mattered.

She wasn't at all surprised to see Pammy already at the pavilion. On the other hand, seeing her sitting with two boys was quite the surprise. Not just one, which would be a little weird, but two boys—that was weirder than weird. The boys had their backs to her. One of them was really tall, even while seated, with dark hair. The other fella, sitting a bit closer to Pammy, had long, light brown hair and was stockier than the tall boy.

Rebekah's stomach quivered as she approached them. Pammy had never walked out like that, much less gone up to the pavilion without her. She must be super mad. Rebekah couldn't blame her. Their summer beach vacations were hardly living up to the much touted "best times of their lives."

Maybe Pammy was just as happy—or happier—to be there with two presumably cute guys than she would be to have Rebekah join them. She turned around and headed down to the water. Her happy place.

I wish I thought to pick up my diary. On second thought, how could I even put into words what happened with the parents and then seeing Pammy? I'm not at all in the mood to meet any new guy, and here's Pammy with two. I've got a lot to figure out if I'm going to have anything close to a good time this week.

She knew that was wishful thinking. Everything had come to a head in that kitchen, and there was no ignoring it or pretending it didn't happen or waiting until they got home to get it settled once and for all. No, there was no going back.

The warm breeze picked up, causing the pampas grass spread out among the dunes to gracefully sway back and forth. Rebekah always loved the pampas grass. It grew and grew. It knew it belonged right where it was. It was unfazed by the scorching heat. It could handle droughts and storms, even hurricanes. Its roots went deep. She could learn a lot from pampas grass. Maybe she was beginning to.

It seemed to her that she had dealt with heat, drought, and storms aplenty over the last year. She would have to investigate how she could relate this to roots growing deep. Rebekah had been so deep in thought that she hadn't realized just how far she had walked. Looking at the pier, right in front of her, brought an interesting realization to mind. She had never even walked up on the pier before. She must have thought of it as a place for grown-ups, not kids, not teens. Which didn't even make sense because she had seen every age imaginable up there, even babies. Not like they were there of their own volition—great word—of course!

Other than a few fishermen, the pier was deserted, and no one stood near the very back of it. Exactly what Rebekah was looking for and needing—total isolation. The breeze at the back end of the pier was noticeably stronger. And the stronger the breeze, the stronger the salty aroma. Rebekah breathed it in so deeply and for so long that she made herself light-headed, sparking her wild imagination.

What if I fainted and fell over the railing? I wonder how deep the water is right here. Would I be able to swim to shore? The water's calm, so I probably could. But what if I couldn't? What if I drowned, and my body just went out to sea? Unless one of these fishermen noticed me—and I'm pretty sure they all have their eyes glued to the water below waiting for the big catch that they could add a few inches to when describing it to friends—nobody would have any idea what happened to me.

Her entire body shuddered at that thought. Pammy would have to find a new best friend. Maybe one of the guys she was with had a sister she could get to know. No, that was stupid, they wouldn't ever see each other again. Sheila could be Pammy's new best friend. She was popular and invited them to her party. What would her parents do? Boy, oh boy, would they ever feel terrible for the way things were left.

Life is strange like that. While we are living, we get mad and stop talking and sometimes never make things right or at least not for a long time, and then things never go back to the way they were. Or it's just too late because somebody dies. Like when Grandma died. I heard Mama tell Daddy that there were so many things left unsaid between her mother and her, and then it was too late. If only it was as simple as not getting mad and not going without talking. But the truth is, it's not that simple, and sometimes whether we like it or not, we just can't stop living exactly like we are. Life dictates life.

Rebekah was giving herself a headache. It was time to get off the pier. No wonder she had never gone up there before. It was so depressing. And the fishy smell—yuck. That just might be her first and only visit.

Before she made her way off, she stopped at the spot she figured was close to where the chain-smoking woman, wearing the ugly sun hat, had hugged the strange man—almost exactly one year before. She imagined a beach full of people walking, running, and sitting under large umbrellas, convinced that, if that was her mother—and she knew it was—she in no way would have noticed that Rebekah was among that crowd. Even if she knew Rebekah was there somewhere, which of course, she did not.

"Jealous of You"

She sighted Pammy well before she reached the pavilion. She no longer sat with the two boys from earlier but stood eating hot dogs with a girl Rebekah didn't recognize. Pammy didn't even notice her when she walked right up to them. They were belly laughing about something the weird girl said.

I guess I don't have to fall off a pier and disappear forever to be replaced by a new best friend. Even a weird one. Okay, I don't know for a fact that she's weird, but she probably is.

"Oh, Rebekah, hi. You startled me," Pammy said as she jumped and let out a quick squeal before placing both hands over her heart.

"I startled you? I have never heard you use that word before—ever," Rebekah sniped.

"Well maybe that's because you never startled me before," she responded, to which she and the new weird girl started up again with ridiculous laughter. "Anyway, this is Susan. Susan, this is Rebekah, my friend I was telling you about."

"Hi." Rebekah glanced at the girl and quickly turned her attention back to Pammy. "So, is that what all the laughing is about? Stuff you told her about me?" Rebekah was not concerned with making a good first impression. She was being snarky and knew it.

Susan stepped back a bit, made up a strange excuse for having to go—something about picking up a little girl who shouldn't have been left alone, or some such thing. She scurried off without saying "goodbye" or "nice to meet you" or anything at all.

"Oh, my gosh, Rebekah, could you have been any ruder?" Pammy slowly shook her head, staring at Rebekah with a look of disappointment in her eyes.

"Oh, please." Rebekah rolled her eyes.

Rebekah made her way toward the front of the pavilion to leave. She really just wanted to get out of there. But she couldn't. Not when The Supremes started singing. Especially when it was one of her absolute most favorite songs ever. Alas, she had no choice but to lean on the railing, listen, and sing along to "Stop! In the Name of Love." In true Rebekah fashion, she sang every single word before skipping down the steps and leaving the pavilion behind her, so as not to be tempted to linger there by another of her absolute most favorite songs ever.

Pammy had stayed right by her side the entire time and was still there as they walked toward the cottage.

"So, who were those guys?" Rebekah finally posed the one question she'd been waiting to ask.

"What guys?" Pammy answered.

"I saw you talking to two guys earlier, Pammy. Why are you acting like it's some big secret?" Not being in any mood to mess around, Rebekah just wanted to get to the point. "I came up to the pavilion and saw you sitting with them. You didn't see me even though you were facing me. I couldn't see anything but the backs of their heads. What are their names?"

"Oh, golly, I don't even know. They were just two guys who sat down and talked for a bit. They were nice enough. I can't believe I didn't see you."

"Well, you were pretty much into them even though they were just . . . and I quote, 'nice enough,'" Rebekah shot back at her, making quote signs in the air.

"Enough already. They were really nice. I like them, okay?"

"Did you like either of them as much as Hank?" Rebekah turned to Pammy with raised eyebrows and a slight smile.

Pammy hesitated for a second, glancing away. "I do like one of them, okay? Maybe even the same as I liked Hank."

"Then I have to meet him," Rebekah replied. "To make sure that he, like Hank, is good enough for you."

Pammy asked, "Where did you go when you didn't stay at the pavilion?"

"Just walking on the beach. I went up on the pier too."

"Really? Let's go there tomorrow. I like looking down at the water through the boards."

"You can, Pammy. Not me," Rebekah said. "I might faint and fall off."

☙ ❧

Part 2: Summer 1967

"Big Girls Don't Cry"

Pammy went straight to the bathroom while Rebekah headed to the kitchen. She wasn't crazy about being back there, but that's where the food was, and hunger trumped unease. Rebekah simply had no choice. She was going to have to get used to it eventually. Now that they owned the cottage and all. Who knew? Maybe they'd owned it all along. Of course, she knew that just because her parents owned it didn't mean that she did too.

"Oh, my goodness, this kitchen is gorgeous," Pammy exclaimed.

Rebekah squealed as she jumped in place. "Pammy! You really did *startle* me, and no, this is not the first time I have used that word. And this kitchen is not gorgeous. It is a ploy by my parents to start fresh and forget all about last year. About all the stuff that I don't even know anything about. That sounds kinda redundant—another great word, I might add—but my whole life is redundant, so for that reason, I will stand by my words."

"Okay, well . . . I really don't know what you just said, and that's okay, but I can't help it if red is my favorite color. I will try, though, to be sensitive to your feelings and not say too much more about how absolutely perfect it is."

"You're a good friend, Pamela Rose Daniels, and I appreciate that we don't have to always understand each other completely to be best friends, right? I mean, unless you and Susan are best friends now, that is."

"Who's Susan?" Pammy winked and gave her a quick hug. "Now, let's eat."

"I'm going to the bathroom, and then I'll come back and put something together. I don't want to eat in here in case my parents come out of their hideaway and decide to have that talk they've been putting off. I will not deal with all that on an empty stomach."

Rebekah led the way down the hall and turned into the bathroom while Pammy went the bedroom to get ready for bed. It had been a long day for both of them.

Thankfully, Pammy had left the bedroom door open because twenty minutes later Rebekah entered with both hands full of a piled high baking tray. "Voila—I present to you, for your culinary pleasure, an enticing array of delectable edibles."

Rebekah was quite pleased with her presentation and a little surprised that she spoke with her best French accent. *Please do not tell me I am turning into my mother.*

"I could work in an expensive upscale New York City restaurant, if I do say so myself."

The spread featured some of Rebekah's most-loved foods, including her mother's famous fried chicken, which was so perfect that it was enjoyed cold as much, if not more, than hot from the frying pan. That night was no exception. Potato salad was always served with fried chicken during the summer. And almost always, but never at the beach—for reasons unknown to Rebekah—with corn-on-the-cob and green bean salad as well. In the winter, her mother served fried chicken with mashed potatoes and gravy made from the drippings, green beans canned fresh from the garden, and a roll of some sort and always, always with a dessert. One thing was for sure, no matter what Rebekah might be holding against her mother at any given time, she loved her cooking. And she tried very hard not to pick her battles around meals. Her father was right—about this one thing—when he said, "Don't cut off your nose to spite your face." It took a long time for Rebekah to understand that was not meant to be humorous. Or literal.

"What is that pink stuff?" Pammy asked. And as the word *stuff* left her mouth, so did a rather large piece of half-eaten chicken. It was gross and disgusting and hilarious. Of course, they laughed until their sides ached. Rebekah was reminded of the laughter earlier that evening that had bothered her so. *How stupid. I should know by now, if Pammy is around, there will be laughter.* It's just that the two of them hadn't enjoyed much of that for a while. Hopefully, that would change soon.

Once they collected themselves, Rebekah told Pammy she was surprised when Pammy correctly guessed the name of the fluffy pink dessert.

"Pink Stuff? That's really the name?" Pammy eyed the blob in the dish.

"That's what my daddy always called it. His mom used to make it every Thanksgiving. That's pretty much the only time we have it too. I don't ever remember having it in the summer. And definitely not here at the beach."

Rebekah, once again, silently questioned her mother's motives. There seemed to be some sort of pattern. Whenever Rebekah brought up that which her parents were determined to ignore, her mother fixed something extra special that Rebekah loved most. Did she think that would make Rebekah forget all about it? How . . . why . . . would she even think that? Oh, well, since she probably would never be able to figure out or understand her mother, she decided to just enjoy.

She was glad that she had spotted the best part of the Pink Stuff concoction on the kitchen counter. As Pammy started to dig into the big bowl, Rebekah stopped her. The mix was fine just as it was and if one didn't know better, they'd just eat it as it was . . . fruit cocktail, pineapple, mandarin oranges, maraschino cherries, and cool whip. Her dad said his mom always used whipping cream instead, but Cool Whip was one of the coolest—pun intended—inventions ever. What would one possibly need to add to that? Rebekah picked up the bag of marshmallows and poured the remainder of the bag into the bowl, mixed well and gave Pammy the go-ahead. "Now."

Although her parents had eaten a small amount of the fluffy, fruity sensation, the girls had nearly finished it all off when Rebekah groaned in discomfort.

Rebekah mumbled, "I am done. I may never eat Pink Stuff again as long as I live. I'm gonna go brush my teeth and go to bed. Let's hope for a better day tomorrow."

"I don't know why, but I'm pretty sure it will be," Pammy replied, stuffing another big spoonful of Pink Stuff into her already full—of Pink Stuff—mouth.

They had been in bed about ten minutes when Rebekah whispered to Pammy, "Are you still awake?"

No reply.

She had something really important to talk about. She had heard her mother crying when she was brushing her teeth. She had never heard her mother cry before. She didn't know grown women cried—unless someone died of course. And even if some women did cry, she couldn't imagine her mother being one of them. But then again, she couldn't imagine her mother chain-smoking and hugging strange men either. She kept thinking . . . *You don't know your mother at all, Rebekah. And she doesn't know you either.*

❧ ☙

Sunday, July 9, 1967

"I Had Too Much to Dream (Last Night)"

An overcast morning was not going to spoil their plans for the day. Well, they didn't really have any plans except for the one. Even if they had to lie out on the beach in the rain. They would do what they had to do to soak up all that was left of the beach life that summer.

Since she had hardly slept, it was not at all hard to get up; don her bathing suit; grab a tote; and fill it with the last of the chicken, some Cokes, and all the usual items. Pammy, of course, had not awakened, so Rebekah gave serious thought to an apropos wake-up song. *Apropos* . . . she learned that word last year in French class. Of course, the French spelling is *á propos*, which looked cooler in writing but was basically pronounced the same.

Not wanting to waste any time, Rebekah tapped Pammy on the shoulder and waited for her eyes to open. One more tap did the trick. She began to sing, "At Last . . ."

"At last, my love has come along? What does that have to do with anything?" Pammy asked as she pushed herself up to a sitting position.

Rebekah was impressed that Pammy knew the song and some of the words. "The guy you met last night. The one you liked as much as Hank. Well, Hank's not here but that guy is so . . ." Rebekah sang the first line again, "At Last . . ."

"Whatever. Maybe you'll meet your "At Last" today," Pammy suggested.

"No." Rebekah shook her head with force. "I already did. And I will never see my Johnny Bean again."

"Which reminds me, you have never told me where that name came from," Pammy retorted.

"Let's go. I'll tell you on the way. It's early enough for us to get our usual spot before anybody else gets there." Rebekah strode out of the room and to the front door.

They didn't start talking until they crossed the street that led straight to the strand. Rebekah had been deep in thought, as was the norm, and Pammy was still trying to wake up, also the norm.

"Okay, so why Johnny Bean?" Pammy broke the silence.

"It's very simple actually. He's sweet. Or at least he was last summer. I guess he still is. But how would I know? I will never know. Oh, man, here I go. I wasn't going to talk about him so that I wouldn't think about him . . . and vice versa." Rebekah groaned.

"Okay, he's sweet. But I still don't get it."

"Like Jelly Bean—only Johnny Bean. You know I give nicknames to all my favorite people."

"I'm sorry that you won't ever see your Johnny Bean again, Rebekah."

"He can still be one of my favorite people, right?"

Yay. No one was sitting in their original perfect spot. She marched straight to it and pulled her beach towel out of the tote. Just as she was reaching for the radio, Pammy touched her arm. "Don't you want to go back where we were yesterday? I like that spot better, and you said you do too."

"I said that because I didn't think we would get this one back. But now we did . . . so . . ." Rebekah completed her task, placing the radio next to her towel.

"I know . . . I just . . . I just like that other spot better. Can we just try it again today and then decide for sure?"

It seemed to Rebekah that Pammy was practically begging. She was definitely whining.

"Oh, my gosh, Pammy." She rolled her eyes. "Why do you care so much about a stupid spot? Sometimes, you can be such a baby. Fine. Let's just go up by the sand dune. Anything to make you stop crying like a little baby." Rebekah stormed off without her towel or the radio.

"Can you at least grab that stuff?"

Pammy said nothing in return, Rebekah glanced back to be sure that Pammy had indeed collected everything. She could not help but notice her friend's stooped posture and her sad demeanor. She guessed that if she could read Pammy's mind, she would know that her best friend was wondering —but would not ask out loud—why the spot that was perfect yesterday was not at all so on this day. Neither spoke as they arranged the area in the same way they always did. They remained quiet as they followed their routine and stayed that way as they settled down to the harmony of The Monkees singing, "I'm a Believer."

Rebekah couldn't keep her eyes open. She'd had another restless night. The dreams never stopped. It seemed to her that she had been awake all night watching some weird psychedelic movie—although she had never seen a psychedelic movie, she certainly felt as though she had last night.

And the star of the "movie" had been her mother. She was eating Pink Stuff and riding down a waterfall on top of a graham cracker. Before she reached the bottom, she flew to a rooftop where she looked down on a group of men, women, and children who were all sitting under bright umbrellas and speaking in sign language. In an instant her mother was sobbing while sitting at the red and white table. She was wearing Rebekah's cameo ring. Her mother then jumped up and ran to give someone a hug. He turned around and told Rebekah that he was in love with her mother. It was Johnny. Instantly her mother was alone again, standing in the middle of the living room of the cottage when she flew up and through the ceiling all the way to Heaven.

If her constant thoughts were exhausting, her vivid dreams were even more so.

༄༅

"Walk Right In"

Rebekah, still lying on her stomach, lifted her head and drowsily asked, "Was I asleep very long?"

"Yeah, for a while," Pammy answered.

"Pammy, I had the strangest dream last night, and I hardly slept at all, and I don't even know what made me snap at you like that. I do like this spot. You don't act like a baby. And I am a jerk and a terrible friend and . . ."

"That's okay. Why don't you just sit up now?" Pammy giggled.

"What's so funny? Am I burnt to a crisp?"

"No, just sit up."

Rebekah pushed herself up. She must still be asleep, dreaming. And this dream was just as crazy—no, even crazier—than the psychedelic one. But way, way better and nothing close to being a nightmare.

It was him! She screamed, she jumped, she threw her arms around Johnny's neck so tight he could barely get the words out, "I was just in the neighborhood, is all."

That was it. No more talk. Not for a really long time.

Rebekah could not stop the flood. Could not even try. It all came crashing down on her. All the confusion, the whole debacle with her parents, the arguments with Pammy, the dreams, the wishing and hoping and giving up and wishing and hoping again and giving up again. She was a bucket of mush.

Johnny sat patiently waiting for her to get whatever it was out of her system. He held her hand and ran his finger over the cameo she wore, as well as her fingertips. Rebekah jerked her hand away, wiped her cheeks, and straightened her shoulders.

"Johnny, I am so sorry. Here I am blubbering all over myself, and I need to tell you how sorry I am about your brother."

She tried hard to keep it all together, but at this, she started up all over again for another two or three minutes.

"It's the worst thing I've ever been through in my life," Johnny said quietly.

She wanted to ask him why he didn't tell her he had a twin, or that said twin was in Viet Nam. She wanted to ask him why he had lied to her about his age. She was ready to talk. But none of that needed to be, or should be, brought up at that time.

"Hey, you got any shorts in that bag of yours? A T-shirt?" he asked.

"Uh, yeah—why?" Rebekah wasn't sure what to make of this inquiry.

"Slip them on over your bathing suit. I wanna take you somewhere."

"Johnny, I really don't want to go back to that place," she insisted.

Johnny shook his head. "No, no, not there. We're gonna get some breakfast. There's a new diner a couple blocks from here, and I'm starving."

Thank goodness. Rebekah's stomach growled, making her realize just how hungry she was.

Hank and Pammy had been having their own conversation and had decided to go for a walk on the pier. Pammy picked up all their belongings, and she and Hank headed in one direction while Johnny and Rebekah headed in another.

As they walked away, The Shirelles finished singing "Soldier Boy."

☙ ❧

"Laugh, Laugh"

The torture from the aroma of bacon and fresh coffee along with the sight of piled-high pancakes and waffles was almost more than a person could endure. Endure they would because every table was occupied, but the thirty-minute wait would surely be worth it.

Ironically, although Rebekah had thought of little else other than what she would say to Johnny if she ever saw him again, she was so nervous she dared not attempt speaking, knowing she would just trip all over her words.

Thankfully, Johnny spoke first. As they waited outside for a table to open up, he began. "You know, Rebekah, I've never met a girl like you before. And I was determined to see you again, somehow. I'm amazed that you are here at the same time as last year. Me too for that matter. Mostly I just really, really wanted to see you. But I also want—uh—need—uh—to tell you the truth about some things, is all."

"Johnny, your table for two is now ready" the hostess called out.

Rebekah wasn't expecting to be called in so quickly, neither was she prepared for Johnny's sober conversation starter. Once they were seated, she started to reply but instead picked up the water glass that the waitress had just set down in front of her. Her throat had closed up, and her stomach churned in anticipation of where the conversation was going. And then it suddenly occurred to her: *Okay, he lied about his age. No big deal, so did I.*

Finding it more endearing than ever that he would think of this little white lie as something to carry such guilt for, she finally spoke. "You know, Johnny Bean, I already figured out that you lied about your age. It's not a big deal. Really. I lied too. When you guessed that I was sixteen, I just let you believe that I was. I wasn't. But I am now, so no harm done."

He looked at her for a long time without replying.

The waitress had set their coffee orders on the table, but neither of them touched the mugs. Since Johnny was making her nervous again, Rebekah turned her full attention to doctoring her coffee. Lots of cream and three spoonfuls of sugar. Stir. Sip. More sugar. Stir. Sip.

"Excuse me, ma'am. Can I get some more sugar, please?"

Johnny's eyes had already gotten bigger with each spoonful, but he laughed out loud at her request for more.

"What?" Rebekah glanced up at him.

"Here you go. Enjoy," the waitress said with a smile. She was not only pretty but pleasant as well.

"I love your dress," Rebekah complimented her.

"Thank you. It's my go-to. The flowers make me happy."

Rebekah was stalling but her compliment was sincere. "Daisies are my favorite flower," she added.

"Mine too," the waitress replied with a smile. "So, are you two ready to order?"

Rebekah ordered two eggs over medium and two slices of well-done bacon and the two pancakes that came with her meal choice. Johnny ordered the all-you-can-eat blueberry pancakes and asked for another pot of coffee.

"So, where should I start?"

"I think we should wait until after we eat, and then we can go for a walk or find a spot on the beach, and we'll talk about whatever you want. Would that be okay?" Rebekah wasn't comfortable with the talk to begin with and certainly not sitting there surrounded by strangers. Especially since it seemed like the whole place could hear them. Johnny agreed but remained deep in thought.

They both dug in as soon as the waitress placed their food in front of them.

It was overly apparent to Rebekah that Johnny was majorly distracted. "WHAT are you DOING??"

"What?" Johnny asked, eyebrows raised and eyes wide.

"You just poured coffee on your pancakes," she said laughing. Despite her inability to stop laughing, she managed to ask, "Would you like some cream and sugar with that?" And she laughed even harder.

"No. I would not. You never saw somebody eat pancakes with coffee?" His hand flew to his chest as if stunned by her question.

"No. Never. Have you?" she asked between laughing and trying to breathe.

"Hmm? I guess not. But I don't know why everybody doesn't eat them this way. You eat pancakes, right? You drink coffee with them, right?" Johnny never stopped eating while talking yet somehow kept his mouth almost closed. Remarkable.

"Yes, I am eating them right now. With butter and syrup. Like a normal person."

"Normal is overrated. You should know that."

"Hey! What is that supposed to mean?" It was Rebekah's turn to feign shock.

For a few seconds they sat quietly, gazing into each other's eyes until Johnny spoke. "It wasn't supposed to be this hard."

"What wasn't supposed to be this hard?" Rebekah asked the question before realizing she didn't really want to know the answer.

As they were leaving, their waitress motioned for them to wait. "I don't ever do this, but I just have to tell you that you are such a cute couple. You look so happy together. I mean, it's the beach, what's not to be happy about, right? But it's more than that. You just look like you belong together. Anyway, I just really wanted to tell you that. Have a great day."

She spun on her heels and headed to the kitchen area. Rebekah met Johnny's gaze. She had no reply. Since he didn't say anything, she guessed he didn't either.

Although the waitress looked vaguely familiar, Rebekah could not remember where she might have seen her. Oh, well. Maybe she'd figure it out later.

"I Want to Hold Your Hand"

It was a rare mild day for Myrtle Beach in July. Not that Rebekah minded the heat, in fact, the hotter the better. But she didn't mind this kind of day either. At least she wouldn't have to worry about sweating—rather, perspiring—as her mother would remind her; ladies do not sweat. Johnny was already sweating despite the nice breeze.

Whether due to too much coffee, too much food, too much laughing, or too much anxiety over what was coming next—or a combination of all four—Rebekah could not ignore the overwhelming need to find a bathroom. Thankfully, she spotted a public one just across the street. Breaking her rule to never use a public bathroom, she told Johnny, "I'll be right back. Just wait here, okay?"

She took off before he could witness the mortification written all over her face. She was gone a good while and was immensely relieved when Johnny neither said anything nor indicated in any way that he thought anything of it when she returned.

Once they started walking, she wanted to tell him that she had washed her hands so he could feel free to take hers in his at any time. Of course, she would never say those exact words, but she did ponder what she could say as a way of hinting that she so very much wanted him to do so. She exercised much restraint by waiting for him to initiate any touch. Girls should never reach for a boy's hand first. But that didn't mean girls should never want to. Once she boldly asked for a kiss, and now she was too nervous to touch his hand. Clearly, much had changed. But what and why was unclear.

"Let's head down to the beach and find a spot to hang out for a while," he suggested. He did not take her hand then or during the entire walk to the quiet spot close to some sand dunes, one of which was home to a pair of discarded flip flops. Another displayed the remnants of someone's unfinished lunch. They settled down a little way from both. Rebekah was certainly disappointed that no handholding had occurred, but mostly she was confused.

He used to like her. A girl knows when a boy likes her. He made a point to find her again. He seemed to very much enjoy surprising her. They had a perfect breakfast together, even laughed with each other. She only hoped that he would finally explain to her what was going on. And exactly what it was that wasn't supposed to be so hard? She was ready to hear it all.

Ready may be a bit overstated, perhaps willing was the better word.

"Where Have All the Flowers Gone?"

Rebekah thought she might burst wide open if Johnny didn't start talking. He sat, staring at nothing, saying nothing. She wondered if he was thinking nothing as well. Absurd idea. Nobody can think of nothing. Even when asleep, people's minds kept working. Granted, some work a bit more intensely than others. She determined to sit quietly as long as was necessary. She would not speak first. Johnny was the one with much to say, so she would wait. But after several more minutes, she thought . . . *If he doesn't say something in two minutes, I will have to. Or I can just leave. I don't want to leave.*

"I love the Eagles," he blurted.

"The bird? That's your favorite bird?" Rebekah asked, unsure what this had to do with anything, but relieved that he was finally talking.

"No, not the bird," he said, chuckling. "But speaking of favorite. I have something for you." He reached behind and pulled it out from under his shirt, "I don't know exactly what a daisy looks like, but this kinda looked like what was on the waitress's dress."

He handed her the flower he had picked while she was in the bathroom. All Rebekah could manage through her weepy eyes and crackling voice was, "My new favorite flower is the black-eyed Susan. Thank you, Johnny Bean."

He smiled the sweetest smile that made her want to tell him how much she loved him. Instead, she simply smiled back.

"I love the Philadelphia Eagles. And I love the Phillies. And the Seventy-Sixers," he explained.

"I don't know what any of that is." Rebekah stared at the delicate flower in her hand.

Johnny chuckled again, only louder. "They are Philadelphia's football, baseball, and basketball teams. You want to know why I love them?" He had stopped chuckling.

"Of course." Rebekah wanted to know everything about him.

"Because I love Philadelphia, everything about it, and I love this country and everything about it too—well, almost everything. Sports represent everything great about our country. Anybody can grow up to be anything they want. Anybody can grow up to play on the best teams in America. America *is* the land of opportunity. It's not just cliché. Too many people in too many other countries don't have any opportunities at all.

"That's a great word—cliché. So, is that what you want to do, play a sport some day in Philadelphia?"

"Well, sure, that would be amazing, but that's not why I'm telling you this."

She did wonder why he was, but she liked this better than what she had anticipated him telling her. Not that she had any ideas per se, but she could not help but sense that it was something that would be hard to hear, whatever it might be.

"I'm not sure I want to know why you're telling me this," she responded.

"I still have to." He took a deep breath, straightened up his back, looked directly at her and blurted, "I am nineteen years old, Rebekah!"

Rebekah's throat tightened as she tried in vain to swallow. In that moment she understood he was relating the fact that while he told her he was a year younger than he was, she told him she was a year older—and he had done the math. She sighed but gave no response before he continued.

"I'm too old for you. I wanted to hold your hand so bad walking over here, but it's not right. I've wanted to kiss you ever since we sat down here, and that's definitely not right. I'm just too old for you, and now I know that you're not even seventeen. You seem older than that. Gees, Rebekah." He ran a hand through his hair.

He did want to hold my hand. He does want to kiss me! Both thoughts made her tingle inside.

She was crying now. She didn't care if he was three years older than her. When she was twenty, he'd be twenty-three. What was wrong with that?

"That's not all I need to tell you though." Johnny's eyes shimmered.

"Is it about your twin brother? I am so, so sorry." Rebekah touched his hand. The excitement of the small touch sent sensations through her whole body. Thrilling sensations she didn't know existed.

"It is, but in more ways than one. I had pretty much already decided what I was going to do after Robby died. I knew I had to. I waited a year because I just couldn't hurt my mom like that so soon after losing him."

Where is this headed? Why do I care so much about this guy? Why couldn't I have been born three years earlier?

"I don't understand why you came this summer just to tell me you're too old for me and whatever other bad things you haven't said yet." Tears poured down Rebekah's face. "It would have been better if I just never saw you again. I would eventually forget about you but now . . ."

"I'm really sorry. Now that I'm here, I know I shouldn't have come. It was a really selfish decision. I just hated the way I left last time, is all. Not that I had any choice, but for some stupid reason, I just couldn't forget about you. But I should have. It's not fair to you," he kept babbling.

"You know what, Johnny Bean? I don't think either one of us is going to forget about the other." Rebekah sniffled and swiped at her wet cheeks while reversing her earlier statement.

"I joined the Army, Rebekah. As soon as I get home, I leave for boot camp and eventually Viet Nam."

She sat motionless for several minutes. He might as well have slapped her in the face. The sting of his declaration, along with the pained expression on Johnny's face as he stared at her, were more than she could handle. She could not compose herself. She had to get away. From the nightmare. From him.

She—like the flower she clasped in her hand—had begun to wilt.

"I can't do this." She leapt up and raced off before Johnny could answer.

◦◦◦

"I Call Your Name"

She ran as fast as she could back to the cottage. *Please, please tell me you remembered your diary.*

If the car or her parents were there, she didn't notice. She swung the screen door open so hard it came off the hinges. All she could think was that she desperately needed to find and pour her heart out to her other best friend. The one that never talked back. The one that only listened.

It was tucked in the pocket of her suitcase along with several pens, pencils, and crayons. Writing pads and coloring pages had long ago been left out of her packing routine. Why she still packed crayons, she didn't know. Maybe because she wanted something that never changed to be a part of her beach trips. Goodness knew, everything else certainly had.

She propped her pillow up against the solid wood headboard of the full-size bed that she and Pammy had slept in all those many years. Before this week, she could have said that at least the cottage never changed. But the renovated red and white kitchen made that claim impossible.

Pen in hand, date entered and thoughts swirling, she began to write. Seven words—that was it: just seven words.

◦◦◦

This Diary Belongs To:

Rebekah Louise Lang

ENTRY DATE: Sunday, July 9, 1967

I
STILL
DON'T
KNOW
HIS
LAST
NAME!!!

She closed the diary; tucked it back in its safe place; replaced the pen, pencil, and crayons; and returned to the bed where she lamented into the pillow that had held so many of her tears over the years. She fell asleep adding to that number.

The room was still bright with the late afternoon sun when Pammy banged the door entering the room. Dramatically flinging herself onto the bed and staring up at the ceiling, she wailed, "Oh, my gosh, I am so glad that's over."

"What do you mean?" Rebekah welcomed the distraction.

"Whew. It took him all day to finally say it and—"

"What are you talking about, Pammy?" Rebekah interrupted with the same question, worded a bit differently.

"Hank and I don't like each other. I mean we like each other. But just as friends—friends who probably won't see each other ever again."

"Why? How did that happen? Give me details. I need details." Rebekah needed to focus on Pammy's startling news as long as possible. A soft knock on the door thwarted her efforts.

Rebekah's mother cracked open the door and peeked in.

"Your daddy and I are going to try the new diner. Come with us," she insisted. "We heard it's pretty good."

Rebekah shook her head. "I will never eat there again," she announced, somehow managing to hold back the tears threatening to overflow again.

"Oh, you've eaten there?" Her mother raised her right eyebrow. Rebekah never understood how she lifted just one. "Was it a bad experience, honey?"

"It was one of the best experiences I will ever experience . . . ever," Rebekah mumbled, unable to hold back the torrential tears a second longer.

Her mother rushed to the bedside and pulled Rebekah into her arms. She did not ask questions; she did not offer comforting words; she simply held her tight as Rebekah rested her head against her shoulder, soaking the sleeve of her mother's pink silk blouse.

She softly, almost silently, called out his name.

"Who Am I"

Somehow Rebekah successfully convinced her mother to go without them, assuring her that all would be okay. "Period stuff. Girl stuff, you know?"

Her mother promised to bring back cheeseburgers, French fries, and milkshakes, the tried-and-true antidote to cramps and mood swings—neither of which was the cause of Rebekah's affliction at the moment.

Pammy would say that was lying, and Rebekah was finding it harder and harder to disagree. But lying or not, she absolutely could not talk to her mother about anything that was going on.

Where is Pammy anyway?

She did not want to get up to find out. "Pammy," she hollered. "Pammy!"

"Good grief, you scared me to death," cried Pammy as she burst through the bedroom door. "Are you okay now?"

Rebekah studied her friend a moment. Her eyes were red and puffy too. *Had she cried for her? Or about her own stuff?*

"No, but you need to finish telling me about you and Hank."

"Nothing much to tell. We just finally admitted to each other that we just want to be friends. Beach friends, you know, nothing mushy."

"That doesn't make any sense. I've seen the way you look at each other and stuff. He's not joining the Army, is he?" Rebekah asked, halfway serious.

"What? No. Not that I know of." Pammy cocked her head. "Why would you ask that?

"That's what Johnny did."

Pammy's mouth and eyes rounded. "He did?"

"Yep, and he's going to Viet Nam too," Rebekah answered, with no emotion.

"He is?" Pammy plopped down on the bed. "Gee whiz, Rebekah. Why aren't you with him right now? I can't believe you aren't spending every single second together."

"He doesn't want to. He thinks he's too old for me. He's nineteen. We'll never hold hands again. He will never kiss me again. I'll never see him again. Crazy, huh? You and Hank decided to be beach friends, and Johnny decided not to be friends at all." Rebekah flung an arm over her eyes.

"What are we gonna do the rest of the week?" Pammy wondered out loud.

"I guess you and Hank can still hang out. I'll just have to remember what I did BJB."

"B . . . J . . . B? B . . . J . . . B?" Pammy pondered.

"Before Johnny Bean," Rebekah enlightened her.

"Ah! Of course. I'm starving . . . you?" Pammy asked.

Rebekah appreciated the change in subject. Kind of. "The parents are bringing us something from the diner. Johnny and I went to the diner for breakfast this morning. It seems like forever ago now." Just then she remembered. "Oh, no."

"What? What's wrong?" Pammy put her hands on her hips.

"I lost the flower he gave me. It was a black-eyed Susan, and it was beautiful, and I lost it."

Rebekah hadn't cried in the last little bit, but her eyes filled and began leaking again, making her wonder if she'd ever be able to stop completely. *I wish I would never cry again. I absolutely will never fall in love again.*

The girls left the bedroom as soon as they heard Rebekah's parents driving up. "Let's sit here in the living room to eat. I just can't go into that kitchen. I'm not sure I can even eat anyway."

Rebekah sat cross-legged on the worn red Davenport sofa, and Pammy sat on the other side of the room in the newer golden yellow swivel chair. She did enjoy a good swivel. Rebekah's father placed the bag of food on the coffee table close to Rebekah and headed for the bathroom while her mother handed them milkshakes—chocolate for Rebekah and strawberry for Pammy, their favorites. Rebekah's parents always remembered all the favorite foods of both girls. Which was but one more reason that Pammy always felt kinda like a second daughter—even if Rebekah sometimes felt like she wasn't their daughter at all. After last summer, Rebekah said she was pretty sure that she had been switched at birth.

"The diner is nice," her mother said. "It's cozy and cute and great service. Our waitress was a very sweet young lady. If you decide to go, be sure to ask for her. Her name is Susan."

Did you already forget that I said I will never go there again? Hmm? I wonder if Susan is the girl that waited on Johnny and me?

And then, just like that, her brain switched gears. "Mother, I have a question for you," Rebekah called out to her as she was heading for the bedroom. Her mother stopped, without turning around or responding.

"Do you ever talk to Vonnie Ella?" she asked.

Rebekah ignored Pammy's raised eyebrows and her decision to opt out of the conversation by swiveling to face the wall, taking her TV tray with her.

"What? What do you mean, Rebekah? Of course I talk to Vonnie Ella. Why are you asking me that?" Her mother had turned around and taken a few steps back toward the living room.

"I mean, do you know anything about her? Her family? Or colored people in general?"

"I must say, Rebekah, you do ask some of the strangest questions at the most unusual times. Are you feeling all right? Do you need something for the, you know, the monthly cycle? I can get you some Midol, dear." Her mother's brow furrowed, and her mouth turned down in a frown. Rebekah recognized the look from lots of mother-hovering moments.

"No. The burger and fries are taking care of that. It's a simple question, Mother. What do you and Vonnie Ella talk about?"

"I should have known as soon as I became 'Mother' again that you were in another snit. I will not fall prey to your nonsense again, Rebekah. Good night."

Pammy swiveled back around to face Rebekah.

"Hmm? We are going 'round in circles again. It seems to me that was quite an overreaction to a simple question," Rebekah said, thinking out loud.

Her father stepped out of the bathroom and offered a cheerful, "Good night, young ladies. I shall retire to the bedroom for some much-desired reading. Enjoy those burgers and the rest of your evening." He didn't ask Rebekah how she was feeling.

As soon as the bedroom door closed, Rebekah concluded, "I guess she didn't mention our little mother-daughter moment. Or she did, and he figured, rightly so, that it won't last."

Pammy peeked over the top of her cup, noisily sucking the last of her milkshake. "Sometimes I don't know who you are. 'Rightly so'? Who says that? Sometimes you act a lot older than sixteen, Rebekah."

"That's what Johnny said too," she answered.

"Have you actually ever seen your birth certificate?" Pammy asked.

Maybe Rebekah had finally convinced her friend to believe that Rebekah may have been right about the whole switched-at-birth thing. It does happen, or so she'd heard or probably read in the *Reader's Digest*.

ಙ ಜ

Monday, July 10, 1967

"Daydream"

Rebekah slept until nine. She hadn't done that since she was a little kid. Her internal clock always went off anywhere from five to six thirty every morning—never later. And for the first time in a very long time, she didn't remember any dreams.

How strange that I would sleep so well after the worst day of my life. I must have cried myself into a comatose state.

She was up and dressed before realizing that Pammy wasn't in the bed or in the bedroom. Muffled voices coming from the kitchen drew her in that direction. She stopped just around the corner to hear who was talking and what—or who—was being talked about. All she heard was suppressed laughter. *Why is Pammy hanging out with them? And what are they laughing about?* She rushed into the room that she could no longer avoid. But only because she had no choice.

"What's so funny?" Rebekah glanced at her parents briefly, then fixed her accusatory gaze on Pammy.

Her father spoke up, "Pammy is entertaining us with her family stories. Her brothers and sisters are quite the characters."

"Sit down, and I'll fix some breakfast." her mother motioned to her. Rebekah made eye contact with her long enough to notice how exhausted her mother looked. Her eyes were puffy, and her usual soft and bright complexion had a sallow look to it.

I guess Johnny and Pammy are right. How many sixteen-year-olds have the word "sallow" in their vocabulary? How many actually work to increase their vocabulary? Why do I? Why am I thinking about that right now?

She felt physically ill just seeing them. The three of them being all chummy. Her mother looking sick. Her father acting like it was just a big party. Pammy entertaining them.

She ran. Again. It was all just too much. Again. She wished she could run into another dimension, another world. One where her parents were just her parents, with no secrets. One like the one she and Pammy had lived in before last summer, one where she had never met Johnny and only liked Mark.

Instead, she ran to the only choice she had in the world—to the beach. After grabbing her diary and pen—never mind whether it was a favorite one, no time for pickiness—she ran to the beach to spend time with the one and only person who seemed to have a handle on reality—herself.

She returned to her new favorite spot for a reason. Maybe, just maybe, Johnny would come looking for her. Which was kinda dumb since he knew exactly where her cottage was if he really wanted to see her. Much to her dismay, she doubted he did . . . want to see her, that was. Plus, he'd have no reason to think she wanted him to since she had run away from him just yesterday.

Right after Christmas, she had put the new diary aside until just the right time to start using it. She had hoped to fill the pages with colorful descriptions of the many daydreams that would be coming true. She couldn't wait to write, in her best penmanship, the details of how she had grown to believe that she did love Mark. That the whole Johnny thing was long over . . . almost as if it never happened. Most of all, she thought about how fun it would be to write and write about the best summer vacation ever. The summer of 1967.

With pen to paper, she began to clear her mind. The words were nothing like she had anticipated. It was not fun to write them. They were not at all about the best summer vacation ever. It was painfully clear—that was never going to happen.

※

This Diary Belongs To:

Rebekah Louise Lang

ENTRY DATE: Monday, July 10, 1967

Only my second entry in this diary and I wish I could write all the things that I was hoping to. How can one person's life be so messed up? Good grief, I'm only sixteen years old, for gosh sakes. For gosh sakes—sounds like my dad. Need to stop saying that, even if I do only "say" it in here.

Well, Johnny and I are over—if we were ever anything at all. I thought we were, but he's decided he's too old for me. Besides, he's going off to war as soon as he gets back home. I don't care how many times I say that, it just doesn't seem real. One thing I know for sure, it is time to move on from Johnny. It's over. It's done. At least I still have Mark.

BUT I'D RATHER HAVE JOHNNY

And then what just happened with my parents and Pammy. Since when have they been all chummy with each other?? It was like being in a "Twilight Zone" episode. Some things just aren't meant to be and one of them is for my parents and Pammy to be all like best friends. Gross!!!!

Mama looked a little strange. Like pale or something. Oh, well, I'm sure she's fine.

I think I do want to see Johnny again.
I know I do!!!

⊱ ⊰

"Lies"

Just as she finished writing, she looked up to see Pammy carrying her tote and a paper lunch bag.

"Your mother made us some grilled cheese sandwiches."

Rebekah said nothing as she pulled one out. It was still warm. Grilled cheese sandwiches —yet another one of her mother's specialties and another one of Rebekah's favorites. Her mother always used just the right ratio of butter on the bread and cheddar cheese between. She always made them with her homemade sourdough bread, and she always grilled them to the ideal crispness, allowing the cheese to melt to perfection. Rebekah rarely ate just one.

Pammy pulled out the other three, holding them up. "Two each," she explained with a huge grin, as she took a big bite.

They ate in silence until all that was left was the four squares of waxed paper in which her mother had so carefully wrapped them.

When she was little, Rebekah watched intently as her mother wrapped her father's sandwiches for work. She would place the sandwich exactly in the middle of the waxed paper she'd laid out on the kitchen counter. Then she would lift both long sides up and fold them together over and over until the folded edge laid against the sandwich. The ends of the waxed paper would then be folded into each other to make a point which was then folded and tucked under the sandwich. She told her mama it was like she was wrapping a present for her daddy, to which her mother replied, "That's exactly what I am doing. Sending daddy off with a present every single day of the week." Rebekah wondered if her daddy really thought of a sandwich as a present. She sure didn't. Not then. But that day it did kinda feel like one.

"I think this is the best grilled cheese I ever had," Pammy said as she balled up the waxed paper and placed it in the paper bag. "Is there anything your mother can't do?"

"Let's just lie here a while and wait for our food to settle and then, if you think you're ready, we can get out in the water for a while." Rebekah hoped Pammy was indeed ready.

"Sounds good. I'm ready." Pammy swallowed so loudly Rebekah heard it.

"Good. I'm proud of you," Rebekah replied enthusiastically.

They lay on their backs for a while with no music.

"Okay, let's go. Ready?"

Rebekah didn't wait for Pammy's answer. She jumped up and ran as fast as she could, shallow-diving into the bluish-green tepid water. The way it hugged her so warmly, it seemed to her that the ocean missed her as much as she missed it. She could not remember a time when she didn't love it. To stay away from it for so long had not been easy. Thankfully, Pammy was finally ready. *Oh, my gosh, where is Pammy?* Starting to panic, she felt a hand around her arm.

"Pammy, you did it!" she screamed.

"I'm doing it, but I'm not loving it."

"We don't have to go any farther out than this; that's fine," Rebecca reassured her.

Just being back in the water was all Rebekah needed. She was perfectly content to remain at the waist-high level. Pammy began to relax too.

But as wonderful as it was to be back in the rippling waves, it was not enough to clear Rebekah's jumbled mind.

"Oh, Pammy, I have so much to figure out. I have no clue how to though. I think I want to talk to my parents about everything. I really need them to explain what's going on. I'm going to be totally reasonable and mature. Did they say anything at all to you this morning?"

"Not about any of that stuff. We really *were* just talking about my family. Stupid stuff. I don't know why they found it so funny." Pammy bounced lightly with the small waves that barely reached her underarms.

"Probably because you have so many kids in your family. I'm sure they wish I wasn't the only kid they ended up with."

"You know that's not true. Your parents are way, way cooler than mine are," Pammy's voice cracked. "My parents don't even care when I'm sick."

"Are you?" Rebekah asked.

"Am I what?"

"Are you sick?"

"No, not really." Pammy averted meeting Rebekah's gaze.

※

"Talk To Me"

By the time Rebekah returned to the cottage late in the afternoon, she had determined that it was time to address the entire situation. She had no idea how but decided to assure her parents that she was ready to sit and listen and do so respectfully. She was just too tired to keep running away from everything and everybody.

She had asked Pammy if she knew where Hank might be so she could hang out with him for a while. Pammy convinced Rebekah that she would figure something out.

As soon as Rebekah crept into the cottage, she heard voices. She had wondered, when she read about the technique several few years ago, if she would ever need to implement it. She took a deep breath and exhaled. She repeated this exercise twice more. If ever there was a time to remain calm, that was it.

After putting her diary back in her suitcase, she did one more breathing exercise before entering the kitchen. She found her parents sitting at the new table, playing cribbage. They could be found playing any number of card games on any given day. Even at the beach. Their idea of a fun vacation must be doing whatever you could to remain bored.

It was hard to tell if they were more shocked to see Rebekah before dinnertime or to witness her sitting down with them. Their eyes rolled toward each other as her mother stiffened in her chair. Rebekah had an epiphany—her mother was getting ready to bolt, just like Rebekah did whenever trouble was before her. It came as no surprise to Rebekah to realize in that moment that her mother's idea of trouble was her daughter—Rebekah Louise Lang.

"I was hoping we could sensibly discuss the issues we've been avoiding for so long now. I am sixteen, and I've been told by more than one person that I am more mature than my years. I am ready to listen."

Rebekah didn't mention that the two people who proclaimed this were not much older than her. Although now that she thought of it, she did have a few teachers who voiced their delight with her extensive vocabulary. She even overhead her father from time to time bragging about how smart his little girl was. She supposed she knew from a fairly young age that she wanted to be an English teacher because of the comments from him, her teachers, and some of her friends—if she could consider Johnny a friend. Friend or not, he would always be one of her most favorite people.

Her mother sat back in her seat, apparently willing to stick around, at least for now. But she was certainly not relaxed. How could any of them be? The firestorm that had been building for so long—although the "heat" was currently being held at bay—was bound to produce some sparks sooner or later.

Rebekah's father scooted his chair back. "Perhaps I should leave you two alone to talk."

"No, Lawrence. I need you to stay here with me. With Rebekah." She glanced at him before turning her attention directly to her daughter.

"We should have done this long ago. I'm so sorry, honey, for having put you through so much. I've just been so afraid of alienating you, disappointing you . . . or losing you forever. I have always been overjoyed by our close relationship, and when it was clear that it had been damaged, because of me, I just didn't know how to fix it. I do now. I'm just going to tell you the truth. You certainly deserve it."

Rebekah was quiet for a few minutes. She wasn't dreading what she would hear. In fact, just the opposite. She was relieved to finally be at this place. Her mother was right about alienating her daughter and disappointing her, but she didn't think there was anything her mother could say that would cause her to lose Rebekah for a long time or forever. She wasn't quite ready to voice that though.

"Daddy, do you know about what I saw on the pier last summer?" She had said "Daddy" without even thinking about it.

"Yes. I do," he answered her question with no elaboration.

"In all fairness, Rebekah, your daddy did not know at the time. I have since explained everything to him." She placed her hand on his, adding, "He needed to be the first to know. To know that he married someone who held secrets."

Rebekah's guard was up now. Her father *had* known, at least for a while.

"So, you're okay with her smoking and hugging strange men?"

"Your mother will explain everything to you. Just as she did to me," he told her.

She folded her arms. "Okay then, I will sit right here and not say a word while you do just that."

"I don't really know where to start. Lawrence, can you help me please?" Her mother's voice shook.

Her father rubbed her mother's hand softly. "It's okay dear, just start. I am right here with you," he assured her.

I think I'm starting to regret this decision.

Her mother took a deep breath and began, "First of all, smoking is not a big deal. I only smoke when I'm under a lot of stress. Which, I will admit, is often. That is nothing new to your father. The most difficult thing that I have dealt with is one that I have kept secret from both of you. I told your father last year when things here at the beach became so tense. I knew I needed to tell you, Rebekah . . . I just didn't know how."

Her mother took another deep breath. "Here goes . . . Sweetheart, I had a baby when I was sixteen years old. My parents made me give him up for adoption. The boy, the father, never knew about the baby. My parents took me out of school until the baby was born and then had me change schools. Everything was kept secret. That sort of thing would have ruined my father's career. It's just the way it was. It was never spoken of again. Ever. I tried to talk to my mother about it before she died, but she refused to acknowledge that it even happened. I was an utter failure in their minds. My father even blamed my mother for my choices."

Rebekah didn't know how or whether to respond. The news that her mother had given birth to a baby when she was her own age was not something she had conjured up in her imagination. Pretty much everything else, but not that.

"The young man you saw me hugging on the pier is him . . . the baby I had thirty-two years ago. His name is Allen."

The three of them sat in silence while Rebekah processed the bombshell. Did she feel sorry for her mother or upset with her? Did it matter how she felt? Was there a right way to feel about that kind of thing? She hadn't read about this type of situation before. Maybe somebody should write about it. Like maybe write a manual on how to feel when you find out that you are not the only child your mother has given birth to. *Maybe I am not her child. That's not so hard to believe now. Maybe I was adopted to make up for the son she had to give up.*

"Am I even your daughter?" she asked, looking from one to the other.

"Of course, you are," they answered in unison.

Her mother added, "After having a baby at sixteen, I was told that damage was done and that I would never be able to have more children. I couldn't believe it when I got pregnant with you. We were elated. Having you, sweetheart, was the joy of my existence. Still is." Her eyes filled with tears at this final pronouncement.

The conversation continued well into the dinner hour. Rebekah learned much more, some of which she had not even wondered about. Some, besides finding out she had a brother, that shocked her.

She had wanted a sibling for as long as she could remember. Being with cousins and friends who had brothers and sisters always reminded her of how lonely she was. Meeting Pammy was the next best thing to having a sister of her own. She didn't know what she would do without her.

Her mother told her that Allen was married and had an eight-year-old daughter and five-year-old son. What her mother didn't mention, though, was that she was technically a grandmother, never mind that Rebekah was not just a sister, but an aunt as well.

By the time Pammy returned, her mother had pretty much told Rebekah everything. She answered all her questions and asked Rebekah a few too. So did her father. There was one question that Rebekah didn't ask because she just didn't want to know the answer.

Her diary would be hearing about it all later.

Tuesday, July 11, 1967

"Soldier Boy"

"I want to see Johnny again," Rebekah told Pammy after they completed the daily setup ritual and she had finished singing with B. J. Thomas. She had loved B. J. since the first time she heard, "I'm So Lonesome I Could Cry." The song spoke to her. She had been lonesome her whole life.

But she felt relief for the first time since she could remember. She would feel even more so once she had a chance to write in her diary. That day was a new day, and they still had most of the week left. She wanted to see Johnny even if he didn't want to see her.

"Wow, I thought you'd want to talk about your newfound brother," Pammy answered.

"No, not really." Rebekah sighed. "It was a huge shock for sure. I'm so glad that I finally know what was going on all this time. Mama says I will meet him. Last summer was the first time she met him. He found out who she is somehow and found her. I don't know anything about how that all happened though. But what I do know is I really want to see Johnny. I just want to see him once more before we leave. What did you and Hank do yesterday?"

"We didn't," was all Pammy said.

"Huh?"

"I didn't see him. I have no idea how to find him. I don't want to find him," Pammy adamantly replied.

"And why is that?"

"Well, it wasn't exactly the whole truth when I told you we decided to be friends. Turns out Hank has a girlfriend . . . has had one for almost a year. He only likes me as a friend, which is fine because I sure don't want my first ever boyfriend to be a guy I only see at the beach sometimes. That would just be stupid. Anyway, he said we shouldn't hang out alone because that was like cheating on his girlfriend. Can you believe that?"

"Maybe he likes you more than he wants to say. Who can understand how guys think anyway? Who would just go marching off to war if they really thought about it?"

Rebekah lay on her back to brainstorm with herself. "I have to figure out how to somehow see Johnny. I'm afraid something will happen to him—like his brother—and I just have to see him again. I just need to lie here and think for a while. No talk, no music." She figured Pammy would oblige.

She was right. Pammy let her know she was going for a walk. When Rebekah sat up after what seemed a good while, she was surprised to see that Pammy was still standing at the edge of the shore. She was holding a huge conch shell to her face and Rebekah could see her lips moving.

She laughed out loud. "Oh, my gosh, Pammy, you are such a kook. Most people listen to seashells, not talk to them." *But you are not most people, are you?*

Rebekah reached into her bag, pulled shorts and a T-shirt over her bathing suit, and walked away, leaving her belongings unguarded. She ran back to retrieve her wallet. She was on a mission that would require it.

At the pavilion, she walked straight to the juke box. Twirling the knob around and around, she took her time finding the songs she wanted to hear. Dropping the coins in the slot, she selected one after another, in just the right order, starting with "Summer in the City."

In keeping with this new phenomenon, she just wanted to listen to each song, not to sing along. No one else was there. She could have—there was a time when she would have—sung as loud as she wanted. But she didn't want.

"It's in His Kiss" followed. Then "Emotions" and finally "Soldier Boy." All the songs she had heard when she was with him. All in the same order in which they heard them.

She returned to the jukebox to play one of them a second time. She cried through the entire song . . . the last one they had heard playing the day before. She had no idea then that she would be told soon afterward that he, Johnny, was now one of them—a soldier boy.

"She's Not There"

The "Please Seat Yourself" sign, positioned just inside the entryway, along with the sparsely occupied diner allowed her to make her way to the exact table she was hoping to find available—the one where she and Johnny sat the morning that seemed so long ago.

Rebekah had never eaten by herself before. At least not in a restaurant. She ate more meals alone at home than she could remember.

One of her recurring dreams was of her sitting alone at a large school cafeteria table. The other tables were full. Kids were even standing up to eat because that was better than sitting with her.

She never saw herself as someone who would eat out alone in real life. But there she was. And it was okay because she needed to talk to Susan. To find out what it was about them that made her comment as she did. That, and she was really hungry. And she'd wanted another chocolate milkshake since the one the other night.

A waitress came out of the kitchen, stopped to fill up a couple of coffee cups, and scurried over to Rebekah's table. Now that she was standing beside the table, Rebekah saw that the waitress was considerably older than Susan. Her dark hair was pulled back in a tight bun and covered with a hairnet, and she was wearing enough makeup for three people. She had a motherly vibe, but not like Rebekah's mother. Her mother only wore a touch of blush and lipstick. Maybe it was more like a grandmotherly vibe. Rebekah wouldn't know since she never met either of her grandmothers.

"Hey, sweetie, are we waiting for someone else to arrive?" she asked in a very Southern accent.

"Uh, nope, just me." Rebekah wanted to ask for Susan but didn't want to be rude.

"Oh, Okay then. My name is Wanda." She pointed to her nametag. "I'll be serving you today, so, what can I get you to drink, sugar?" She smiled pleasantly through cigarette-stained teeth. Rebekah hoped that wouldn't happen to her mother's teeth.

"I would like a chocolate milkshake. Extra whipped cream please." Rebekah always asked for extra whipped cream. She could probably drink a whole glass of it and just skip the milkshake part, but she had never had the nerve to ask for it. Besides, she had always been with her parents when she ordered one, and her mama would have been mortified. Although, she suddenly realized, she could try it sometime at the Dairy Queen. Or at home, for that matter. She gave herself a mental pat on the back for such a brilliant idea.

After the waitress returned with her milkshake and after she had taken her order, Rebekah figured she could at least ask about Susan. Maybe she could speak with her for a minute before she finished eating.

"Is Susan working today?" she asked.

"Hmm, I don't know a Susan," the waitress replied.

Wanda must be new. "Oh. She served my friend and me the other morning. I was hoping to speak to her for a minute."

"We don't have anyone by the name of Susan. Do you mean Sharon? She's in the back. I'll get her for ya."

"That would be great. My mother must have misheard her name, is all." Rebekah could not believe she just said, "is all." Just like Johnny did. How odd. Or not. It should be no big surprise since he had gotten into her head—and had taken up residence there since last summer.

Wanda delivered the cheeseburger and fries and let her know that Sharon was finishing up something and would be right out.

She was halfway through her burger when she looked up to see Sharon heading her way. Sharon was definitely not Susan. Sharon was not blond, not thin, and not particularly pretty.

Sharon was very nice though. Older folks were quick to remind young people like her that was so much more important than how one looked. *Yeah, well, tell that to all the boys, would you?*

"Hi, there, honey. I'm Sharon. Wanda said you wanted to speak to me."

"I'm so sorry. I was looking for Susan. Wanda didn't know who that is. I'm guessing that you do."

"No, sweetie. I've worked here since we opened, and we've never had a Susan as a waitress." Wanda scrunched up her mouth. "What does she look like? Maybe we can figure this out," she offered, eager to help.

"She's really pretty. Medium-length blonde hair. Not real short or real tall. She was wearing a super cute dress with daisies on it. I remember, because daisies used to be my favorite flower. Now it's black-eyed Susans." Rebekah felt stupid for saying the last part. At least she stopped herself before telling her how Johnny was responsible for the switch. But saying it out loud gave her pause. Black-eyed Susan? How strange, what was it with "Susan" already?

"Well, I don't know what to tell you, honey. Your description just doesn't match anyone who works here. I'm sorry, sweetie, I sure hope you find her though. Maybe it was a different restaurant, huh?"

It was not a different restaurant.

She had one more place to go. It would be hard, but she needed to go. If she could find it that was.

"I Remember You"

She had been in a daze and paid little to no attention to where they had walked after breakfast. She hoped—and said a little prayer—that she could remember where they sat.

Glancing at the black-eyed Susans as she passed by, a reluctant smile appeared as she imagined Johnny tucking the flower behind his back. She crossed the street at the corner just as they had done. But that was as far as her memory could take her.

She had been so caught up in handholding—wanting to that was—that she had paid no attention to where they walked or where they ended up. She did recall one thing, so on that tidbit, she tried retracing her steps. Within a few minutes, she was standing in front of one of the many sand dunes that, for the most part, all looked the same. Except for the one—the discarded flip-flops had not yet been retrieved, thankfully.

That was it. The last place they were together. She sat down to reminisce. She could imagine him sitting there. His gorgeous green eyes with those ridiculous long, dark eyelashes. His amazing thick, almost-black hair, once again blown about by the soft breeze off the water. His beautiful hands. She had always been fascinated by boys' hands. Johnny's were perfect. Long fingers—she called them piano fingers. Just a touch of dark hair on each one. Johnny didn't wear any rings, and his fingernails were clean and clipped to a nice length. Rebekah made a mental note to never bite her nails again. She knew a girl at school who twisted a strand of hair around her index finger over and over again. Maybe she would try doing that whenever she was tempted to place a fingernail between her teeth. A few dead ends wouldn't be nearly as disgusting as ten nubby fingers.

Years ago, she had replaced thumb-sucking with nail-biting, so she knew change was possible if she put her mind to it. She sucked her thumb until she was ten years old. Never in front of others, only at bedtime. When she was about five or six, a friend of her father, whose thumb had been cut off down to the knuckle, showed it to her and told her it was from sucking his thumb. You would think that would be all it would take for Rebekah to stop right then and there. But Rebekah was not one to give up so easily when it was something she wanted. To make such a rash decision on the spot would be silly. Thus, for several nights at bedtime, she compared the thumb she sucked against the one she did not. Seeing no change in its length or structure, she would fall fast asleep, doing what she had done for as long as she could remember, thankful that thus far she had gotten away with her thumb intact.

She could almost hear Johnny talking about things that made no sense to her. He might as well have been speaking in French. She made a good grade in French, but she certainly didn't remember any of it. Well, not much of it. Now she wished that was all they talked about. Sports and stuff she had no clue about.

She wished he wasn't nineteen. She wished he wasn't old enough to go into the military. She wished he wasn't old enough to go to war. But he *was* nineteen, and he *was* old enough to join the Army, and he *was* old enough to go to war. Nobody should be old enough to go to war.

War was yet another thing—like treating coloreds different from whites and starving people in the world—that she would never understand. And she never wanted to. To her, injustices should always be seen but never understood—in the sense of agreeing with them, in the sense of supporting them. Why anyone would support the idea that certain people are less worthy of human rights than others was beyond her. Who decided those things anyway?

The pins and needles in one of her legs demanded that she stand for a while. Rebekah straightened her leg and wiggled it around before she leaned over to pick up a wrapper lying next to her foot. While she would be hesitant to pick up someone else's discarded lunch, she was certainly willing to throw away a bit of candy wrapper. One touch and she knew it was not a candy wrapper at all.

How was it possible that it was still there? It was as if it had determined that, while it may have withered and died there, it was not going to be buried there as well.

☙ ❧

"I Say a Little Prayer"

Rebekah slowly sloshed her way along the water's edge to where she had left her things, figuring Pammy would be there soaking up some rays.

Pammy was there but not just soaking up rays. Rebekah approached the three of them with no fanfare. No throwing her arms around his neck. No crying. No relief. But definitely surprised and somewhat nervous.

She stood over them, eyes locked with Johnny's as he maneuvered his long legs to make room for her. She wasn't sure whether to sit across from him or somewhere else. That decision was made for her when she realized there was nowhere else for her to sit. And she really needed to sit, wondering if he noticed her shaking legs.

As awkward as it was, Rebekah was beyond thrilled to be with him again. No amount of brainstorming on her part had led to any ideas of how to make what had happened happen. Maybe she thought by retracing yesterday's time together, she would run into him doing the same. How silly. Guys didn't do such things.

But that wasn't the only reason she went from place to place. She did it in case she never got to see him again. At least they would have spent one last afternoon together, albeit without his even knowing. She opened her hand to show him the pitiful little flower. He offered her a slight smile as his tilted head and questioning eyes told her he was unsure what that meant.

"It's the one you gave me. Can you believe I found it right where I dropped it? Pretty crazy, huh?"

"Where *I* dropped it . . . actually. I picked it up after you dropped it and then dropped it again before I left," he told her.

Pammy stood up. "I'm going back to the cottage to get something to eat."

Hank took the opportunity to pretty much say the same. Rebekah debated whether to stay where she was or move to Pammy's vacant towel. Her wise inner voice won the argument. As she scooted over, she half expected Johnny to leave too.

"So, what did you want to ask me?" he said, his voice soft and mellow.

"Huh? What do you mean?"

"Pammy said you had something really important to ask me," he replied.

Rebekah didn't ponder long before realizing . . . *Of course she did. Only Pammy could scheme this well. She knew I was sick about it and took it upon herself to save me from my own stupidity.*

"Oh, yeah, I kept meaning to ask you, and somehow I got sidetracked every time—"

"I have a question of my own, well a couple of them actually," he interrupted.

"Exactly," she exclaimed. "You see how quickly the conversation goes in a completely different direction?"

"Sorry, you first. I won't forget *my* questions." Johnny's teasing smile alone had the power to get her off the subject, but not again. She was determined.

"What's your last name?" she asked.

"Rizzo. What's yours?"

"Lang." And after a short pause, "Johnny Rizzo? Sounds like a movie star. Are you a movie star, Johnny Rizzo?" she teased.

"Nope. Not yet anyway."

"Okay, what's your question?" Rebekah was eager to hear what

Johnny could possibly want to ask her. At least she now knew, as she had hoped, that he had been thinking of her.

Johnny busied himself with brushing off the sand that had accumulated on his legs, as he confessed, "I was wondering if I could give you a nickname too, is all."

"Well, that depends. Is it because you give all your favorite people nicknames?" Rebekah gave him a teasing smile in return.

"It is now, Rebekah Sue."

Rebekah had been fooling herself by trying to be sensible and realistic. Telling herself she was way too young to continue on this path to nowhere. Convincing herself they'd never see each other again, never mind be together in any real-life scenario and that she'd be okay with that.

None of that mattered one little bit. Johnny leaned close and broke his own rule. It was a real kiss, not just a slight touch of their lips. And she kissed him back.

Rebekah silenced those practical voices and turned up the volume on the irrational ones. She was too young—too young to allow worries about the future to rip the present right out from under her. The plain and simple fact that they were crazy about each other made loud and clear the voice of truth . . . no amount of avoiding each other would change that.

They would no longer avoid each other, quite the opposite in fact. They would spend every possible minute together from then until Saturday morning.

*Please make time stand still . . . now **that** would be an answer to prayer.*

"Barefootin"

"Pammy, you are a genius. It took me a minute, but I realized exactly what you meant when you told Johnny I had a question." Rebekah had run into the cottage to give Pammy the biggest hug she had ever given anyone—except Johnny. "You are brilliant and the best friend imaginable. I love you!"

"Well, it was pretty obvious you were never gonna find out on your own," Pammy said as she laughed.

"We are going to see each other as much as we can. Which means, we need to get ready to go to the pavilion right now. Oh, my gosh, I feel like a new person. Like the real me." She slipped the pitiful flower into the suitcase next to her diary. It would be fine there for a while. Rebekah did not consider for one moment that a dead flower was not a suitable representative of her relationship with Johnny. She considered it exactly as it was, a beautiful little flower that her sweet Johnny Bean wanted her to have.

Little time was spent getting ready. She wished she had a dress with black-eyed Susans on it, but the short baby blue shift with the cute little blue and white rope belt that made it even shorter, was a good choice. Her mother got most of her clothes from the Sears and Roebuck Catalog because the size three always fit Rebekah perfectly, length and all. There weren't very many reasons to appreciate being an only child, but having one's choice of clothes was one for sure.

Poor Pammy had to wear hand-me-downs. And not just from one older sister. She had to wear her older sister's older sister's hand-me-downs. Whenever something of Rebekah's fit Pammy, she would let her borrow it. That night was one of those times. Rebekah thought Pammy looked better than her in the pink and orange Mod Flora dress anyway. She would probably give it to her. Pammy's boobs were bigger than hers, and the empire waist called for an "ample bosom"—that's what her mother called it. Rebekah would never say those words out loud.

They managed to sneak out before her parents came back from wherever they were. Rebekah didn't care anymore. She had been set free from trying to catch them in their lies. She felt kinda bad now that she knew what it was and why it had been kept from her. She still wondered about a couple of things. Things she was in no hurry to find out about.

Pammy told Rebekah she wasn't sure that Hank would be there, but if he was, she hoped it wouldn't be awkward. She was totally fine with him having a girlfriend even though the whole cheating thing was a bit ridiculous. Unless there was actual cheating going on. Which there wasn't. Hank had never even kissed her.

Rebekah only heard about half of what Pammy said. She, herself, was very nervous. Although she and Johnny had spent at least an hour together talking after the amazing kiss, doubts began popping up as the pavilion came into view. Not about her own feelings, but about his. Had he come to his senses again? Had he reminded himself of the reasons why they shouldn't be together? Would he be there at all?

She needn't wonder for long. Johnny watched and waited for her by the front rail next to the steps. Rebekah's legs went weak again at the sight of him. She wondered if he felt the same. He looked incredible in his white button-down shirt—his muscles tight against the short sleeves—and dark jeans. It wasn't just her looking at him. She noticed quite a few of the girls checking him out. Why wouldn't they? He may not have been in any Hollywood movies, but goodness, he sure looked the part. Like James Dean or Paul Newman handsome.

He held his hand out as she reached the steps. He didn't say a word while he led her onto the dance floor. "Dance With Me" had just started. Had he somehow arranged for it to play as soon as she walked up? Or was there some higher power at work? Is that what prayer was all about?

Never mind all that. I am dancing with the best-looking guy in the whole place, and he is looking at me like, well, like I thought only happened in books and movies. Or only to me in my imagination and dreams.

She had slow danced one other time before Johnny, and this was already the second time with him. That first time, before Johnny, shouldn't even count because it was part of the fifth grade "Dance Around the World" class that was required once a month as part of her school's physical education program. Every boy was embarrassed, and every girl wished her partner was anybody but who it was. Rebekah could slow dance no better now than she did then, and it was pretty bad then. Not as bad as square dancing but pretty close.

But Johnny was such a good slow dancer that he basically made her a better dancer than she really was. She hoped he made her kiss better too. She wasn't about to ask him if that was the case, as much as she'd love to know. He knew she had never kissed anybody before last summer, but what he didn't know was that she and Mark had done plenty of kissing since then. Johnny was a way better kisser than Mark. While she had yet to slow dance with Mark, she was pretty sure that Johnny was way better at that too. Wow, that was the first time she had thought about Mark, and it was to compare him to Johnny. That was so unfair. No other guy could compare to Johnny Bean. Poor Mark.

Rebekah kicked her shoes off and finished their dance on her tippy toes. She was five feet six to Johnny's six feet, and the pumps had just enough lift to allow her head to rest at his shoulder. Without them, their embrace took on a "Mutt and Jeff" feel.

"These pumps were killing me," Rebekah complained, shoes in hand, as soon as they sat down with Pammy and Hank. She was afraid it might happen—new shoes did that sometimes—but they were just so perfect with her dress. Simple little pumps, the exact color match to the blue in her dress. She had to take her chances. Actual blisters were so much worse than hypothetical ones—*hypothetical*, one of the words from last month's *Readers Digest*. Rebekah wondered how many new words she had learned just from doing the "It Pays to Increase Your Word Power" every month. And again, she wondered why she would think of that in such a moment.

Back to the present, she noticed that Hank looked lost and hadn't said anything at all. Rebekah felt bad for him. He was not at all like the Hank they met last summer. Not that he was super talkative then, but he was at least a part of the group. He seemed a million miles away or at least however many miles it was from Myrtle Beach to Philadelphia.

"Hank, what's your girlfriend's name?" Rebekah asked, attempting to bring him back in.

"Huh? Oh, me? Uh, her name is Sarah," he answered.

Johnny leaned over and whispered to Rebekah.

Rebekah stood up, grabbed Pammy's arm and pulled her along. "Pammy, we're going to the bathroom."

"Johnny just told me that Hank is afraid that you're uncomfortable around him since he has a girlfriend. So, either you need to reassure him that you are fine with it, or he's gonna leave, and then it will be you, me, and Johnny, if you know what I mean."

Pammy scrunched up her nose. "Fine."

☙❧

"I Think We're Alone Now"

Johnny held her hand snuggly in his, carrying both their shoes with the other. As they reached the shoreline, he dropped her hand, placed the shoes in that hand and gently took her other one to lead her around to his right side.

"Why did we do that?" she asked. "Is this a new dance step?"

"My dad taught me to always walk on the side of any potential danger when walking with a girl," he explained.

"Are we in danger?" she asked, unable to imagine what that might be.

"Well, if a tsunami hits, I'll be the first to go, is all." Johnny chuckled.

"Oh, my, I am with a very chivalrous fella. And he uses big words like *tsunami* too. Be still my heart." She squeezed his hand. Her heart was anything but still.

"So, how many girlfriends have you had?" Her question came out of nowhere. Seemingly so, but she had been dying to ask him since that first little peck of a kiss last summer. She finally decided that since there probably was no perfect time, then there was no time like the present. Now that she knew just how amazing his kisses were and how good he danced, she almost didn't want to know the answer. Almost.

"None," he answered, with no indication that he was joking.

"You don't really expect me to believe that do you?"

"Well, I've never lied to you before this, so why would I start now?" He rubbed his thumb on the back of her hand. "Well, except for the whole age thing."

"Okay, so how come you dance so good?"

"I have two older sisters who have been teaching me since I was about ten years old, is all," he explained.

That made sense, but she still wondered how he learned to kiss like he did. For sure, he wouldn't have learned that from a sister. She wondered if he was going to ask her about boyfriends, which thankfully, he did not. She also wondered if she would have lied.

They hadn't meant to walk all the way to the pier. At least, Rebekah didn't mean to. She was serious when she told herself she would not return there. But when Johnny, holding her hand firmly in his own, made his way toward it, she offered no resistance.

Anything she did with him was all she wanted to do, and anywhere she went with him was the only place she wanted to be. It might as well be the first time she stepped foot on the saltwater-stained boards. The fishy smell was not nearly as bad as she had remembered. The memories of her mother wearing that silly sun hat and hugging the strange man were no longer disturbing ones.

She was still curious about Allen's family and the man who saved Pammy, but even that no longer caused her angst—how she had come to so appreciate that little five-letter word, even though she never got to use it with her parents. If she were to give a title to her life over the last year that word would have to be in it. Like "The Angst of Rebekah Louise," or even better, "The Day Rebekah Sue Said Goodbye to Angst."

She didn't particularly enjoy the feel of the slimy, sticky boards against the soles of her feet, but wouldn't consider putting her shoes back on. Since Johnny didn't move to slip his shoes on his feet, she assumed he felt the same.

Her Keds had gone straight into the washing machine the last time she walked on the nasty boards. Since that wouldn't be an option for his loafers or her pumps, they concentrated on getting to the bench that awaited them at the back of the pier. A handful of fishermen were scattered about.

"You know, we talked a really long time the other day, but you never asked me the other questions you mentioned," Rebekah reminded him.

"Yeah, I've been kinda nervous about that." Johnny pushed his hair to the side again. He had been doing so all the way down the pier. The wind swirled around them. His hair would not stay in place. Rebekah thought about how he wouldn't have to worry about that much longer. Although she couldn't imagine Johnny with shorter—or no—hair, she had no doubt he would be just as handsome without it.

Before she could ask why he was nervous, Johnny spoke again. "As soon as Pammy told me you had a question, I decided to go ahead and ask what I wasn't going to before. I wanted to ask if you would consider writing to me when I'm away. There, I said it."

"So, when did you decide that I wasn't too young for you after all?" she asked.

"I didn't. I still know I'm too old for you. But I'm not listening to my head. I should be, but I'm not. And I'm kicking myself because it's not right for me to ask you to write to me, but that's what I did. This is what I'm doing. And it's not—"

Rebekah stopped him. With a kiss. A kiss that said, "I don't care about all of that. I will write to you. I want to write to you." Although she wanted to keep kissing him, she pulled away. Continuing to kiss and be kissed by him would have said a lot more than was safe, such as "I want to be with you forever. I want to be Mrs. Johnny Bean Rizzo."

This past year, when she thought that she would never see him again, she was glad she hadn't told him she loved him. And now that she heard her mother's story, she realized how stupid it would be to change her mind back to that dangerous territory. She couldn't imagine being faced with what her mother had gone through. *Sure, times are a bit different, but, getting in trouble like that was still very much taboo. How could she put her mother in that situation after she had dealt with so much?*

Reluctantly, she opted for more conversation over more kissing. "Was that the only other thing you wanted to ask me?" Rebekah asked.

"For now. You said you had some questions too," he reminded her.

"I do," Rebekah turned to him with a look of concern and asked, "Why are you doing this? Going to war?"

Johnny walked to the railing, staring out at the ocean. The breeze was no longer swirling but was strong enough now to push his hair straight back, exposing his entire forehead. Rebekah held her hair back with both hands as she moved up beside him. He looked down at her with a concerned look of his own.

"What happened?" She reached up and touched the two-inch scar along his hairline.

Johnny touched it too in reaction to her question. "This? Robby gave it to me," he chuckled. "I used to hate that thing, but now it's a way to carry my brother with me everywhere I go. When we were about five or six years old, we were having a snowball fight. The one that got me right there had a big ole chunk of ice in it. Scared us both to death. Blood everywhere. Robby was scared he'd get in trouble, and I didn't want that, so he ran in and got a big Band-Aid, and somehow, we got it to stop bleeding. I wore my beanie in the house for days to cover it up. My parents just thought I was going through a phase. By the time my mom saw it, it was too late to get stitches, so it's just been this big ole scar since then, is all. My hair's been covering it for a long time, but that's about to change, huh?"

His voice and his eyes drifted off. Rebekah studied his profile as he stared out to sea. The full moon, illuminated across the ocean, seemed close enough to touch. After she glanced around to confirm that the two of them were the only ones on the pier, she began singing the first line of "I Think We're Alone Now."

Johnny smiled and sang the next line. Together, they finished the entire song, continuing to look at the moon and the stars above and the dark blue water below.

"There won't be any tumbling to the ground—or pier—going on here," he mused.

"Something your dad taught you?" Rebekah asked, teasingly.

"Well, yes, but also my Father," Johnny explained.

Rebekah cocked her head. "Your dad isn't your father?"

"See that beautiful moon, Rebekah? The stars that can't even be counted. See the sky? There's no end in sight. Feel that amazing breeze? Look at the water below us. Can you even imagine how many gallons it is?" Johnny turned to make eye contact with her.

"I can't, but . . ."

Johnny placed two fingers gently on her lips. "My Father made all of it. He made me, and He made you. God is my Father, capital *F*, and He taught me that. I care about you a lot, Rebekah. I will never touch you inappropriately. Not that I don't love that song—I do. But it's really important to me that you know that I would never do anything that could hurt you . . . and then, as soon as I say that, I realize I am taking the chance of hurting you just by asking you to write to me. To be in my life. And here I am going to war. I'm kinda messed up about it, is all."

Johnny sat back down, quiet for several heartbeats. Rebekah sat back down beside him but didn't know what to say.

"Do you read the Bible, Rebekah Sue?"

"Not really," she answered.

"Do you have one?"

She shook her head. "No, I don't. Why?"

"Read John 3:16."

"I don't know what that means." Rebekah felt weird about the turn in their conversation. "Johnny, the thing is, even if you told me that you don't want me to write to you after all, even if I had never seen you again after I ran away yesterday, do you really think I would just forget all about you? It's too late for that."

After a few more silent moments, Johnny took her hand and looked at her with a smirk. "Come on, we're gonna do something fun!"

Answers to hard questions could wait. Spiritual quests could be left to ponder silently. The beach nightlife beckoned.

"Mustang Sally"

As soon as they got back to the pavilion, they washed their feet as best they could under the outdoor spigot. He walked Rebekah back to her cottage and told her to get some comfortable clothes on and wait there for him.

"Go see if Pammy is inside and let me know," he said.

Rebekah returned to report that yes, she was.

"Great, I'll get Hank, and we'll be back here in a flash. You two get ready. And no pumped shoes, or whatever you call them."

"Pammy," Rebekah called out. "I sure hope you and Hank are okay, because they're coming to get us, and according to Johnny we're going to do something fun. Something fun, Pammy. This is what we've been waiting for. It's getting just a little cool out, so we should wear jeans and bring a sweater. And tennis shoes." She laughed to herself at the thought of "pumped shoes."

And so, Pammy changed into jeans and a tee and slipped on her Keds. "Me and Hank talked for a long time earlier. We agreed hanging out and being friends is just that—two friends hanging out. We're fine."

Rebekah found her parents in the kitchen playing gin rummy. "Pammy and I are going out for a while."

Her parents barely looked up. "Have fun," Mama said.

Good thing they never worried. Once she became a teenager, her parents basically gave her free reign of the beach. How far could she and Pammy go on foot anyway?

They would have been as surprised as the girls were when Johnny and Hank pulled up to the corner of the narrow street. Rebekah's mouth dropped open. She grabbed Pammy's arm. She tried to speak, but her words were gibberish. Rebekah could not contain her excitement, and she had no desire to try. She squealed and jumped up and down, with no concern whatsoever as to how ridiculous she must have looked to the others. She considered doing a cartwheel but thought better of it. What if she landed wrong and hurt herself? In her wildest dreams, she could not have imagined that she would find herself going for a spin with a guy like Johnny, much less in the car of every teenager's dreams. But there she was being escorted to the passenger side of a 1965 Mustang convertible. No gymnastic move was worth spoiling this night.

"Let's go have some fun." Johnny opened the car doors for her and Pammy. Rebekah wondered if his dad or his Father with a capital *F* had taught him that. Either way, it made her feel like a queen.

"Is this your car, Johnny Bean?"

"I rented it for the night, and I insisted on the Baby Blue color to match your eyes." He didn't give Rebekah time to react before admitting, "Naw, just kiddin'—it's my brother Glen's. He said I could borrow it. First time he's said yes."

"Where are we going?" she asked as soon as he jumped back behind the wheel.

"You'll just have to wait and see, won't you?" Johnny teased.

As far as she was concerned, they could ride around in circles all night, and it would still rank as the most fun she'd ever had. Just being at the beach with her Johnny Bean in such an amazing car. Forget about pinching herself. She needed to leave a bruise to believe this was actually happening. But since she wasn't into self-harm, she'd forget about that too. As hard as it was to believe, it was really happening.

Johnny drove the sporty little car out onto the main highway where the speed picked up. Rebekah was glad she had pulled her hair in a ponytail. Having her hair flying all over her face would have been a nuisance she was happy not to deal with on the most perfect night of her life. *Pammy must have had this in mind when she decided all those years ago to keep her hair short.*

Rebekah focused on Johnny's beautiful hands as he smoothly changed gears with one and gripped the steering wheel with the other. She looked down at her own hands and nails, thankful that she was one day into her no nail-biting plan and hadn't even resorted to hair twisting. She did, however, continue to mindlessly pick at her cuticles.

She wished she'd left her cameo ring back at the cottage. It was starting to feel wrong to keep wearing it, especially when she was with Johnny. She allowed that thought to creep in, but she would not allow herself to dwell on anything but the moment.

And in that moment, she knew for sure what car she wanted. She had hoped to get a car for her birthday, but it was best that she didn't, because who knew what they might have gotten her. Now she could tell them exactly what she wanted—a Mustang. She would be sure they knew she wasn't at all picky about the color as long as it was a convertible, but Baby Blue would be her number one choice if she did get to choose. Rebekah had reluctantly settled for driving the station wagon every chance she got. Surely, her parents would get her a car of her own soon if she proved how responsible she was, not to mention how open she was to every grocery store run that was needed. Neither they nor she had mentioned the small dent in the fender. She hoped they wouldn't because as hard as she was trying to stop lying, she would not hesitate if that's what it took to avoid losing her driving privileges.

The speedometer showed a lower speed than Rebekah thought it would. The wind and the hum of the engine seemed to add the feeling of an extra twenty miles per hour or more. As far as she was concerned, the ride alone was adequate for the fun Johnny promised—and had delivered.

Any conversation was all but impossible and not at all necessary. Rebekah could hear Hank's and Pammy's voices talking nonstop, but she had no idea what they were saying. She began running through a list in her head of guesses as to their destination. The list started and ended with putt-putt golf. But unless Johnny hadn't seen the three courses they just passed, she figured it would remain a mystery. She did enjoy a good mystery.

"What's your favorite animal, Rebekah Sue?" Johnny yelled.

"My favorite animal?" Rebekah wasn't sure she heard right.

"Yeah, what's your favorite animal?" he asked again in a normal voice while sitting at a red light.

"Dogs. I love dogs. I used to have a dachshund, but he got run over by the mailman," Rebekah told him. "His name was Ralphie. Why are you asking me that?"

Johnny winked at her as he took off again. "You'll see."

The mystery deepened . . .

"Far, Far Away"

"Oh, my gosh. I've heard about this place since forever, but for some reason my parents never brought us here. Oh, my gosh, Johnny."

Rebekah practically jumped in his lap as she wrapped her arms around his neck and very well might have if not for the gearshift between them.

"So, I gather you like my surprise." Johnny said, grinning.

"Are you kidding? I love it. Pammy, it's like going to the fair at home but better, huh?" Rebekah turned to the back seat. Pammy nodded.

"I'm starving, and the hot dogs here are the best," Hank offered, hoisting himself up and over the car door.

"Let's eat and then hit the roller coaster," Johnny suggested.

Rebekah was one hundred percent onboard with the plan.

"I'm not really hungry, so I'm gonna skip the hot dog. I'll probably skip the roller coaster too. I read about how old and rickety is. Just doesn't sound all that fun to me," Pammy informed the others.

As the three of them enjoyed the fair food, Rebekah gave much thought as to how she loved hot dogs. Hot dogs were always good, but foot long hot dogs at the North Carolina State Fair and at the Myrtle Beach Amusement Park were, by far, the absolute best. Side-by-side taste tests of Rebekah's mother's coleslaw and the one at the fair, however, would be won every single time by Mrs. Eloise Lang. But without hers to compare, the Myrtle Beach Amusement Park hot dog and coleslaw was an award-winning, mouth-watering delight. The greasy crinkle-cut French fries and Coke made it a meal for the ages. They were a couple bites into their hot dogs when Pammy excused herself to go to the bathroom. Rebekah kept enjoying hers, realizing she probably should have gone with Pammy, as she polished off the last bite. By the time Pammy got back, the others had finished their meals and were gung-ho to hit the midway.

Before standing up from the table, Johnny placed his arm around Rebekah's shoulder, leaned down to kiss her cheek and whispered in her ear. The tingling from his touch, his soft lips against her warm cheek, and his warm breath in her ear surged through her entire body with such force she wondered if it traveled straight through her and back to him.

Rebekah knew that continuing in the direction they were headed was unwise, but she flung those thoughts off. Being together in that moment was their reality. Nothing else existed. No age gap, no worries.

It was just the two of them spending an enchanted summer evening together, doing the things that young lovers did. Laughing, hugging, kissing—and tingling.

Rebekah wanted more than anything to empty her mind and heart of everything except this moment in time. Two lovestruck teenagers, carefree and full of hope for the future. But the stark reality was this: Johnny may be under twenty years of age, but to consider him a teenager was absurd. He was a man. He was going into the Army and he was marching into war.

Still, she determined to push it as far back in her mind as possible. She drew a deep breath, taking in the savory mix of onions, burgers, hot dogs, funnel cakes, cotton candy, and a dozen other carnival scents—each one helping to steady her resolve. The screams and squeals of excited kids and their happy parents, and most especially the way Johnny gazed at her as if they were the only two in the entire park, made it possible to quiet, if not completely silence, the voice of reality.

"I want to do one thing before we ride the coaster," Johnny called out to Pammy and Hank.

"What is it?" Rebekah asked.

"You'll just have to find out, won't you?"

"You do love being mysterious, don't you?" Rebekah laughed, slipping her arm in his.

They hadn't walked far before Johnny stopped in front of a basketball game where he exchanged a dollar bill for five basketballs.

"Three made-baskets wins a small stuffed animal, four wins a medium one, and all five wins a biggon'," the carny called out.

Johnny had his eye on a huge one and told him so.

One after the other went in, not one striking the rim. With each made-basket, the other three cheered him on, growing louder and louder as he sank one after another. By the third try, several onlookers joined their cheering. If any of that made Johnny nervous, Rebekah sure couldn't tell. One-, two-, three-, four-, five . . . just like that, not one miss. He pointed to the prize he'd already decided on. "Give it to the girl with the baby blue eyes."

He turned to her. "It's not your favorite, but it's probably as big as your Dachshund was."

Rebekah hugged her huge stuffed dog. "Did I say Dachshund? I meant Bulldog. I love him, and I know the most perfect name for him. Ralphie. Thank you, Johnny Bean."

Rebekah reached up on her tippy toes to kiss his cheek, taking in the heavenly aftershave and his sweet smile that made his beautiful green eyes sparkle. Oh, how she wished the night would never end.

Hank suggested one more stop on the way to the roller coaster. The four of them, lined up beside each other, picked up their air guns. Hank counted, "Three, two, one, go."

They shot over and over again at the small ducks floating by in front of them. Each of the girls shot three ducks, Hank shot eight, and Johnny twelve. Twelve earned him a small prize—a plastic bag with a set of jacks. He tossed it to Hank. "Here, since it was your idea to play."

Hank awkwardly handed it to Pammy.

Johnny's soft expression hardened, his jaw twitching. "I guess I'll be doing a lot more of that pretty soon. Sure wish I would be only shooting air at little plastic ducks though."

Rebekah turned to study him. "Are you having second thoughts about joining the Army?"

"Nope. Just don't want to go into it with my eyes closed, is all. But let's not talk about that right now. We have a roller coaster to conquer." He grinned at her as if he hadn't just had the sobering thought.

They meandered through the crowd to the foot of the white wooden structure that looked like something any sane person would walk right past.

The screams above them gave Rebekah a chill. Johnny would be trading screams of delight for screams of war. How did a person even do that? How would he?

So much for pushing it all far, far away.

"For What It's Worth"

Rebekah and Johnny scurried from one ride to another, stopping only to indulge in an irresistible treat along the way.

Kissing at the top of the Ferris wheel, holding tight to each other through the haunted house, bumping into mirrors—and each other—in the house of mirrors, all at a whirlwind pace that kept the gnawing thoughts at bay.

When the ride stopped with their chair at the top of their second Ferris wheel jaunt, Rebekah searched for Pammy and Hank below. The couples had gotten separated after the roller coaster. Of course she couldn't spot them among the hordes below. And of course, even if she had, she doubted she would find them once they were back on the ground. She hoped, though, that they were still together down there and, better yet, having at least half as much fun as she and Johnny were.

For the first time since they entered the park, as soon as they got off the ride, Johnny glanced at his watch. "Oh, wow. It's midnight, Rebekah." He furrowed his brows.

"Oh, wow. I've never been out this late before," she answered, not at all worried.

"I better get you back. Your parents are probably frantic. His eyes were huge, and the smile that had been in place practically all night had been replaced by a concerned look Rebekah had never seen from him before. She wasn't sure whether it made her sad to see him like that or impressed by his incredible thoughtfulness.

"Oh, gosh, no; they are probably sound asleep. They never worry about us," she assured him.

"Even so, I should have had you back before now."

They made their way back to the car expecting to find Pammy and Hank waiting for them. Rebekah was glad when they didn't find them there. She didn't want the night to end, and, just as importantly, their unexpected solitude provided the perfect time to delve deeper into Johnny's decision to go to war. Especially since his twin brother died over there. She longed to know his why.

"Why don't you stay here, and I'll go look for them," Johnny suggested.

"I don't want to be here alone. Besides, they might come back as soon as you take off to find them," Rebekah reasoned.

"That makes sense. We'll wait a little while." He clasped her hand and leaned against the hood of the gorgeous car.

"Johnny, please explain to me why you want to go to war. Please help me to understand."

He gazed straight ahead for several minutes. Rebekah had learned from their beach discourse not to rashly speak before giving him the time he needed to respond. Ah, discourse—another great word recently added to her repertoire—ah, repertoire, also recently added.

She spent the several minutes allotted to study his profile again. The way his hair covered all but the right corner of his forehead. Just the right amount of wave to lay nicely across it without covering his amazing long, dark eyelashes. His perfect nose. Very few people had perfect noses, but Johnny Rizzo's could be used in a plastic surgeon's brochure.

Even when he was deep in thought, his dimples could be seen, though they became much more pronounced when he smiled. The cheeks . . . great cheekbones just under his deep set dark green eyes. His lips. Oh, how she did so love his lips. She decided to move on quickly from there to his slightly pointed chin with a small dimple of its own. And the way his hair fell just below his not-too-big ears—well, he was indeed very nice to look at. It suddenly occurred to her that he could not be more opposite of Mark, even in his physical traits. Mark was cute but she would not describe him as handsome. Poor Mark. He had no idea there was a Johnny in her life. For that matter, Johnny had no idea there was a Mark in her life. Truth was, whether she was with Johnny or with Mark, Johnny was always in her life. The same was not remotely close to being true concerning Mark.

Johnny broke her concentration, "I have to . . . I just have to. It's something I can't really put into words. Not any that can explain it. I wish I could give you some answer that would make sense to you. But I guess there just isn't one, is all."

"Is your mother okay with your decision?"

He shook his head. "No."

"Your dad?"

"Kinda."

"Your Father with a capital *F*?"

"I think so. And I don't want for Robby to have died in vain. Maybe something good can come from it all."

Rebekah sat in silence digesting his words. He did have an explanation that made sense to her. Hard as it was to hear, it made some sense. War itself would never make sense, but she supposed the desire to do the right thing always would. Somehow, she was sure that Robby was just as proud of his twin brother as his twin brother was of him.

Was there anything about Johnny that could possibly make her stop falling in love with him?

Wednesday, July 12, 1967

"Wake Up Little Susie"

By the time Pammy and Hank returned to the car it was close to one o'clock. Johnny's concern had turned to anger. Rebekah felt it radiating off him.

"Where have you been, Hank?" Johnny demanded. "Did you bother to look at the time at all?"

"Sorry, man. Pammy got sick after we rode the merry-go-round. I thought she was gonna pass out. Freaked me out." Rebekah could tell by Hank's shaky and high-pitched voice that he was pretty shook up.

"I'm okay now," Pammy said. "It just took me a while to feel better. Sorry."

"Oh, man. No, I'm sorry, Pammy. I shouldn't have gotten so mad.

I just don't want you two to get in trouble for being out so late, is all." Johnny ran a hand through his hair. "Let's just get going."

Rebekah had quickly reached for the passenger door handle when Johnny gently removed her hand to open the door for her. As hurried as he was, he was still first and foremost the epitome of gentlemanly behavior. Her heart swelled as she placed a little peck on his cheek.

He reached into his pocket and pulled out the napkin he had used earlier, handing it to Rebekah. "There's a pen in the glove compartment. Use this to write down your address for me, okay?" His beautiful smile had reappeared. "Grab that Bible too, that's for you to keep."

"This is a Bible?" Rebekah had never seen a paperback Bible.

"Yep, it's called The New Living Bible Translation. It's good for anyone who hasn't read the Bible before. It uses words like we use today, so it's easier for some to understand. I still like my NIV, but I read that one some too," Johnny explained to her.

Rebekah thought the Bible was just the Bible. Who knew there were different ones with different covers and all? She didn't really understand everything Johnny said, but it was sweet of him to give her one of her own. Maybe everybody was supposed to have one.

Johnny drove well over the speed limit all the way, as if getting back at one thirty would somehow be better received by Rebekah's parents than driving up at one forty-five. It was obvious to all of them that her parents had been standing on the cottage steps for quite some time when the Mustang pulled up to the corner. Her parents reached the car before any of the occupants had time to get out.

"Get out of that car right now, young lady, and go straight in the house. We will discuss all this tomorrow. You too, Pamela."

"Dad . . ." Rebekah tried to speak as she let herself and Pammy out.

"Now," her father hollered.

As much as she wanted to stay to explain and, most especially, to defend Johnny, she did not.

She had never seen her father like that. And she had certainly given him plenty of reasons to "put his foot down" in the past. He didn't even raise his voice when she'd snuck out of the house and roamed the neighborhood all night with Pammy. They would have gotten away with it too, just as they had with several other escapes, had they not forgotten to relock the window once they snuck back in. Even so, it had not occurred to her that he checked all the windows every night before bed. Who did that, anyway?

Once, when she got caught in a lie, all he did was tell her not to do it again. The punishment did not fit the crime and so, although she had never been caught again, she did not come close to never doing it again. But she was lying less and less if that counted for anything.

As she turned to leave, she glanced at Johnny. He had gotten out of the car, hovering several inches over her father. He dared not look her way but gave full attention to the man who was demanding it of him.

Rebekah rushed into the bedroom and opened the window as quickly and quietly as she could. She could see all of them. Johnny and Hank stood against the car, her father still positioned in front of Johnny, and her mother stood slightly behind and to the side of her father.

"Pammy, come over here. Maybe between the two of us we can figure out what they're saying." Rebekah scanned the room for her friend.

Pammy lay on the bed and didn't answer. Rebekah pursed her lips and gave a heavy sigh. She turned her head so that just her ear was against the window opening. No matter how she strained to hear, she heard only muted voices.

ಶಾ ಳ

"You've Got Your Troubles, I've Got Mine"

To say Rebekah woke before dawn would be an understatement. She didn't really sleep. She may or may not have dozed a little, but sleep—no. She had been checking the clock all night long, as if seeing the time would coax her to sleep. It had not.

When she was little, she would *try* to stay awake. She wouldn't want to go to bed while watching TV, so she would force her eyes wide open—trying with all her might not to blink—certain that her parents would be convinced she was wide awake. At some point, she would wake up, without remembering falling asleep or being put to bed. She did remember that it was almost painful to keep her eyes open for so long. But that alone did not stop her from trying again and again.

At that moment, she found herself in a precarious situation. She had seemingly had the upper hand with her parents for so long that it hadn't occurred to her that one day it might all change. That day had arrived.

She lay on her back staring at the ceiling. She would let Pammy sleep until seven, and then they would devise a plan. One more glance at the clock indicated that Pammy still had an hour. It must be nice to be able to sleep no matter what. Rebekah wondered if she would sleep just fine if Pammy was the one whose whole life was one disaster after another. Well, maybe that was a bit overstated. Her whole life wasn't, just the part she had no control over.

She began reliving last night in her mind. It was magical. Like a movie. A wonderful romantic movie. Weren't they supposed to have wonderful, romantic happy endings? This one may have already ended—unhappily—at one thirty in the morning.

Pammy cleared her throat and rolled toward Rebekah. "Well, that was a crazy night."

"I'm worried, Pammy. Real worried." Rebekah's voice squeaked as if to emphasize her concern.

"What do we do now?" Pammy asked.

"I say we get out of here while we can. I'll face the music eventually, but I'd rather not start the day that way." Rebekah grabbed the beach bag and gathered her bathing suit and towels.

She tip-toed out of the bedroom and into the bathroom. Once she brushed her teeth and put her bathing suit on, she tip-toed back to the room where she found Pammy ready to go.

"Their bedroom door is closed, and I didn't hear a peep," she whispered to Pammy.

A quick bathroom stop for Pammy, and they would high-tail it out of there, ever so quietly, of course.

"Where are you ladies going this morning?" Her father's booming voice gave them a jolt. He and her mother sat on the porch swing, fully dressed and sipping coffee.

For several seconds, Rebekah was too stunned to speak. Pammy kept her mouth clamped shut.

"To . . . the . . . b . . . b . . . beach," Rebekah stuttered.

"So early?" he asked, but they knew he wasn't expecting an answer. "Don't you want to talk about last night?" Again, probably not really interested in an answer.

"Let's go inside where we can all sit down comfortably and chat," her mother offered.

They were freaking Rebekah out—again. All nicey nice and using such calm syrupy voices. She seriously doubted they used those voices with Johnny and Hank.

Of course the girls did exactly what they were told. Her dad sat in the armchair, the girls on the davenport. Her mother strolled to the kitchen with the coffee cups.

Oh, boy, they're getting refills. This may take a while.

Rebekah dared not look at Pammy.

As soon as her mother returned and sat on the arm of the chair beside her father, he coughed to clear his throat. "You probably think I'm going to yell at you or ground you. Or both. I could do all that, but it's important you both know, as hard as it is to imagine, your mother and I—and your parents as well, Pamela—were young once too."

He took a sip of his coffee. "We remember wanting to have fun and sometimes losing track of time. For that reason, there won't be any punishment."

Rebekah fell against the back of the cushion, stunned. "You mean, we can just go on to the beach and do what we want just like we've been doing?" She shifted her gaze to her mother.

"Well, that's not exactly what I said, now is it?" her father answered, directing her attention back to him.

Rebekah had no clue what that meant but knew it wasn't anything good.

"No, that's not at all what I said," he continued. "While there will be no punishment, your mother and I *will* be keeping a very close eye on you from here on out."

She didn't ask what that meant exactly because she didn't want to know what that meant exactly. And so, she simply nodded and asked if they could head to the beach.

He smiled. "Of course." He picked his cup up again.

Rebekah, followed by Pammy, hopped off the davenport.

"By the way," her father interrupted her escape. "I did have a very nice talk with the boys you were with last night. Nice young men. I told them the same thing I just told you. You girls go ahead now and have fun."

"Wait," her mother said as they reached the door. "Let me fix you something to take with you to eat. It'll just take me a minute."

Rebekah did not intend to stay even a minute more, "That's okay Moth . . . Mama. I have some money, and we'll get something to eat in a bit."

"Oh, Okay. You should go to the diner and ask for Susan," her mother called out to them as the screen door slammed. "She's such a nice young lady."

Yeah, I already did that.

"Respect"

They may not have had any conversation all the way down to the beach, but it wasn't because they weren't thinking about everything that transpired over the past twenty-four hours, particularly the last few minutes. At least, Rebekah was, and she assumed Pammy was too.

Once they were lying on the beach towels and the music was going, the exhaustion set in for Rebekah. She wanted to sing. She wanted to talk about everything. But just like when she was little, she just couldn't stay awake.

Rebekah was awakened suddenly by a crying toddler passing by with his frustrated mother, who fussed at an older kid, who screamed at yet another kid. It felt like she'd been asleep for hours.

She glanced over to see Johnny sitting on a towel next to her and Hank lying face up on his towel next to Johnny.

"When did you get here?" Rebekah asked, sleepy and smiling.

"Just happened to be in the neighborhood, is all." Johnny smiled back.

"I need you to tell me everything my dad said to you," she said between yawns. "I wasn't sure I'd ever see you again. But first, I would like a little hello kiss." She leaned toward him.

"Uh, that would be a no." Johnny pulled away. "Take a look just past my left shoulder." His eyes darted in that direction.

"You . . . have . . . got . . . to . . . be . . . kidding . . . me! What are they doing here?" Rebekah started to jump up and run over to them, but Johnny caught her arm.

"Don't do it, Rebekah Sue. Calm down. It's okay," he assured her.

"There is absolutely nothing okay about my parents spying on me," she insisted.

"Listen, we messed up. I messed up. I get it. They don't know me from Adam. But your dad and I talked a while, and I think he pretty much believes that I'm an okay guy and that I'm not gonna hurt you. Let's just do this his way. If we don't do this his way, we won't do this at all. And I respect that."

Rebekah sighed. Guess she'd respect it too.

❧☙

This Diary Belongs To:

Rebekah Louise Lang

ENTRY DATE: Saturday, July 22, 1967

I've been home a week and I have so much to write about. It's all bouncing around in my head, and I'm trying to figure out how to put it all into words. The most important thing is that even though my parents stalked us like a couple of FBI agents on our trail, Johnny and I still got to talk a lot. He has my address and said he would write to me as soon as he got home. But I haven't gotten anything yet. I should have told him to send it Air Mail. That's how I send letters to my cousin in New York, so they'll get there really fast. I hope I get one really soon. I asked him to send a picture too.

One thing we talked about was when I asked him again about any girlfriends, and he still said he never had one. I don't know how that's possible. He didn't actually ask me to be his girlfriend, so technically I guess he still hasn't ever had one. I think I am though 'cause we talked about some pretty serious stuff. He told me that Frankie Valli had a new song out that was his song to me. I think that pretty much means I am his girlfriend. It's called "Can't Take My Eyes Off of You" and I LOVE IT!! And I LOVE HIM TOO!! I'm gonna buy it today. I will listen to it every single day until the day I die!!!

All the stuff my mama told me was crazy. She said I would probably meet my "brother" Allen before school starts. He lives near Washington, DC. He said he's excited to meet me. He has a brother and now he's happy to have a sister too.

But that's not the craziest thing. She told me he is deaf!! And get this . . . the huge man who saved Pammy from drowning, the one we saw on the beach with his family, the one we saw on the pier "that day"— he's deaf too!! But he can talk and read lips. He's a friend of Allen's and agreed to meet at the beach to help him and my (our) mother communicate with each other. Allen said his name is John, but everybody calls him Big John. That makes total sense. It was all a big shock. Learning about Allen and all of it, but it did make a lot of things come together. I'm so happy about that.

Another mystery was solved too. I asked Daddy about the scratch in the table. He said that he did it a long time ago when he and Mama were arguing. She was upset about something, but she wouldn't tell him what it was. He said that happened a lot and on that morning, he just got way more frustrated by it than usual and picked up the knife and dug into the table. Mama said that she felt that way whenever she thought about the baby she gave up, but she didn't tell Daddy, so they argued. I'm glad that's over now!

Something that I haven't talked to anybody about is how I think something might be wrong with Mama. But I'm not sure, and I didn't even want to ask. It's probably my imagination because she still does everything she always has. It's not like she's in bed all the time or anything. I really don't want to think about it anymore. My imagination gets me in enough trouble.

Anyway, I'm not sure when I'll see Mark. I might tell him about Johnny. Then we'll break up, and I guess I'll have to give him back the ring. But maybe not. Mama told me when you give someone a gift, it's theirs to do with as they wish. She told me that when I found out that Darlene had given Caroline the bracelet that I gave her for her birthday. Darlene said it was because she already had one just like it, but I never saw her wear it if she did. And she wore bracelets every single day. Oh, well!

Gotta go now—Pammy and I are going to see "The Gnome-Mobile." It looks good. My parents are letting me drive us. Then we'll go to a music store and buy the song that was written just for me—tee hee; it seems like that anyway.

I still have to talk to them about getting me a Mustang.

I REALLY MISS JOHNNY BEAN

I need to ask him what his middle name is.

ENTRY DATE: Wednesday, August 2, 1967

I've heard MY song on the radio a few times. It's the most romantic thing ever.

"Can't Take My Eyes Off of You" is the most beautiful song ever written. And the way Frankie Valli and the Four Seasons sing it is just D R E A M Y!

It's driving me crazy that I haven't gotten a letter from Johnny yet. This is torture!

ENTRY DATE: Friday, August 4, 1967

OH MY GOODNESS! I finally got a letter. Mama just came in with it. She said she really liked Johnny and since he was going to war, it would be good for him to have somebody to write back and forth with. Gonna go read it right now!

My hands are shaking!! My heart is pounding!!!

July 24, 1967

Dear Rebekah Sue,

I don't have a lot to say 'cause I've been busy getting ready to head to Boot Camp. We had a big family get-together over the weekend as a sendoff for me.

I leave in a week for Ft. Dix in New Jersey. I'll be there for eight weeks. Not sure where I'll go after that. Not sure if I can even get mail or write when I'm in boot camp, but if I can I will write as soon as I can and give you my address.

I think about you all the time, girl. Especially about what we talked about that day at the pavilion when your parents were sitting on the other side. *Kinda funny now when I think about them following us all over the place. I don't blame them, though.*

What do you think of the bald guy in this picture? HA HA! It feels weird!

I was wondering if you looked at the Bible yet?
Gonna go for now.

Love,
Johnny

જ⚜

This Diary Belongs to:

Rebekah Sue Lang

My new middle name—I love it so much!

ENTRY DATE: Monday, August 7, 1967

So, I've read Johnny's letter over and over. His picture is so cute. Wouldn't you know, he doesn't have big ears even without hair!! It's just like Mary Poppins said . . . He's practically perfect in every way!! He said he thinks of me all the time. I am a very lucky girl!! And he signed it Love, Johnny!!!

Pammy and I went to see "The Gnome-Mobile" (it was kinda good but I kept thinking about Johnny), and then we went to the music store, and I got the record. I've listened to it so much already, I might wear it out and have to buy another one soon.

By the time I got Johnny's letter it was too late to write back to him. Besides, he didn't put his return address on the envelope. I'm glad it still got to me. Or it would have been floating around somewhere . . . who knows where. He must not have learned how to properly address an envelope in school or else he forgot. Or else he was so excited to get it in the mail to me that he rushed it. I like that reason the best.

He better remember to put it on his letter from boot camp, or I won't be able to write him back. I REALLY HOPE HE WILL BE ALLOWED TO WRITE! I think he probably can because that would be so mean if they couldn't even write to their mamas (or their girlfriends)!

Pammy is gonna sleep over next weekend. We will probably walk around the neighborhood and maybe go to the pool. There are lots of kids that we haven't seen at all this summer. I just want to keep busy, so time will go really fast.

I'm gonna go now and listen to my song and read my letter again. Then I'm gonna look at the Bible some. I'm gonna read John 3:16 first. I think that's the one that he told me to read.

ENTRY DATE: Monday, August 14, 1967

Oh My Goodness!!! I have SO MUCH to write about after the weekend. Pammy and I decided to go to the city pool since my parents said I could use the car. That pool's bigger, and the diving board is way better. I love to dive, but Pammy still doesn't know how to swim, so she never dives. I tried to tell her that I could teach her to dog paddle to the edge, but she doesn't want to do anything but hang out in the shallow end. Ever since what happened at the beach, she hardly ever even gets in the water. I wish she would learn to swim, but she's too afraid. I guess I get that. Anyway, I was on the high dive and just before I dove in, I saw him lying on the grass with a girl!! I couldn't believe Mark would do that to me!

I decided to just walk right up to them, and boy, oh boy was he shocked. He didn't know what to say. I have never seen the girl he was with before. Anyway, we didn't even talk, I just made sure he knew that I knew and then walked away. I guess we are broken up now. I'll find out more once school starts. He won't be able to ask for the ring back; that's for sure. It kinda makes me sad but mostly mad. At least I didn't hang out with Johnny right in front of him!

ENTRY DATE: Monday, September 4, 1967

School starts tomorrow. I can't believe I'm gonna be a junior this year. Seems like I just started ninth grade and now I only have one more year after this. I'm ready for school to start, the end of summer gets boring. No more letters from Johnny. I guess he isn't allowed to write after all. And his boot camp is eight weeks long! So if I'm counting it right, he'll be done at the end of this month, but I don't know where he'll go after that. I hope he's okay.

I'm so nervous to see Mark. I don't know what I'll do now. I've been with Mark for so long. Now I don't have an at-home boyfriend to be with. I might have to go out with somebody else, so I don't have to be alone. I mean, Pammy and I will always do stuff, but being with a boy is different and makes you feel special.

I'm gonna wear my white dress with the eyelet collar and hem and my white pumps with the little bow for the first day of school. Mama said there were two reasons why I shouldn't wear that tomorrow. First of all, she said we should never wear white after Labor Day. Well, I want to know why. And who says that we can't? She said that people who know all about fashion say so. I told her since I don't know any of those people then I don't care. Then she said that it looks more like something I would wear to church. And I told her that since we don't go to church, then I would never get to wear it. She didn't say anything else after that.

Speaking of church, I read what Johnny told me to in the New Living Bible he gave me. John 3:16 says, "For this is how God loved the world: He gave his one and only Son, so that everyone who believes in him will not perish but have eternal life" (NLT).

I'm not at all sure what that means. Maybe Pammy and I should go to church somewhere. Some of the kids at school do, so we could find out where and maybe go *sometime*. *She'll probably think I'm crazy. Maybe I am.*

I HOPE JOHNNY WRITES SOON!!

ENTRY DATE: Saturday, September 9, 1967

The first week of school has been pretty good. I didn't see Mark until Thursday since we don't have any classes together. Thank goodness for that. But guess who I do have a class with?? His new girlfriend. She's new at our school this year. She is in my English class. She didn't even recognize me from the pool that day. But I recognized her. Mostly because she's really pretty. She seems to be popular already 'cause lots of girls who were sitting around her kept talking to her. I think her name is Donna, but I'm not sure. When I finally saw Mark, they were sitting together at lunch. Not sure why I didn't see him before that. I still can't believe he hasn't even bothered to talk to me about anything. Like, when did he start liking her? And when was he gonna tell me? Still no letter from Johnny. It is so hard to like a boy this much when you can't even see him. Or even talk to him.

ENTRY DATE: Tuesday, September 12, 1967

I AM SO EXCITED!! As soon as I got home today, I checked the mail. Well, I do that every day, actually. But today there was a letter from Johnny. FINALLY!!

I wrote back to him right away. His letter was SO sweet. I've decided that I don't even want any other at-home boyfriend. I will wait and wait for Johnny.

September 7, 1967

Hey Girl,

How are you doing? I finally got a chance to write. Boot camp is kicking my butt. If I'm not exercising or doing drills or eating, all I want to do is sleep. I got to make a couple of phone calls home. I asked if you had written to me, but nobody has seen anything. Don't write to me at home anyway. Use the address on this envelope.

I got my next orders for training. I'll be going to Ft. Rucker in Alabama for AIT (Advanced Individual Training) to be a helicopter door gunner. I scored high enough to get into that, and I'm super excited about it. So far, I like being in the Army, even Boot Camp. Which tells me I'm gonna like the rest of it even more.

I think about you all the time, Rebekah Sue. Every night when I'm falling asleep, I think about you, hoping I'll dream about you. I haven't yet but maybe tonight I will. Don't forget to send me a picture as soon as you can. I want to stick it up on my bunk.

Hope to hear from you soon. You'll have to tell me all about school. How's Pammy doing?

I'll write again as soon as I hear back from you.

Love,
Johnny

ENTRY DATE: Tuesday, September 12, 1967

Since I can't keep a copy of my letter to Johnny, and he might lose it in his moves, I copied it here. I hope he gets it soon!

Johnny Bean,

I was so happy to get your letter. I've been going crazy waiting to hear from you. It sounds like you're doing good, and I'm glad about that.

I couldn't write back to you before because you forgot to put your return address on the envelope. Thank goodness you did this time.

School isn't too bad. I like my classes, except English. Well, I like English just not everybody that's in my class. I like most of my teachers.

Pammy is fine. We have two classes together, so that's cool. Last year we didn't have any together.

I bet I miss you even more! I keep your picture on my nightstand and Ralphie sleeps with me every night. I miss you so much.

I listen to "Can't Take My Eyes Off of You" every . . . single . . . day!! More than once.

Do you think you can ever call me? Here's my phone number just in case you can.

I am sending this to you by Air Mail so you get it really fast. Please write or call or both SOON!

XOXO,

Rebekah Sue

P.S.: Here's a picture of me that my parents took with our new Polaroid camera.

P.S.S.: I read John 3:16. Pammy and I are thinking about going to church with some of our friends. What do you think I should read next in the Bible you gave me?

ENTRY DATE: Wednesday, November 15, 1967

I haven't written in here in forever. Mostly because I've been writing to Johnny every night and then when I have a week's worth, I send them to him. He's called me twice. I love, love, love hearing his voice. He said the same about hearing mine. We don't get to talk very long but at least we get to talk some. He will be finished at Ft. Rucker in early December. But I think he said he will go to one more specialized training before Viet Nam. I think he called it Jump School.

Of course, I wouldn't tell Johnny about the whole Mark thing, but it's getting kinda weird. I was in the bathroom at school a while back and guess who came in?? Donna . . . I found out that is her name. She doesn't know that I used to be Mark's girlfriend, so she just started talking to me. It's crazy, but I really like her. She's kinda like me, which is really strange that Mark would drop me like a hot potato to have a girlfriend who is a lot like me. Anyway, since we are in English class together, we realized that we both have this fascination with words. Learning new ones and all. She even likes to do the word power in "Reader's Digest" too. Isn't that C R A Z Y??

I thought Pammy might be a little jealous, but she doesn't act like it. She likes Donna too.

Thanksgiving is coming soon, and we're supposed to go meet Allen and his family. I'm kinda nervous about that. I've never talked to anybody who is deaf. I wonder if "Big John" will be there to help all of us understand each other.

ENTRY DATE: Thursday, February 29, 1968

Okay, so a lot has been happening, and I just haven't taken any time to write in here. But since this is a Leap Year and today is February 29th, it just seems like I should note that. I know I can't remember everything, but I'll try to give a good synopsis (a new word that Donna and I both learned from "Reader's Digest"). She even used it in class, and the teacher was very impressed. Wish I'd thought of it first, though.

Anyway, speaking of Donna, she and Mark broke up. She broke up with him!! She wants to hang around with girls and with boys who are good friends, but Mark gets too jealous, so she said Toodeloo! When I told her that Mark and I used to go together, she said he talked about me a lot, but he never told her we were a couple before.

Johnny and I have been writing. He'll be done with the special training soon and then be heading to Viet Nam. I'm not sure when, but it's getting close. I get a knot in my stomach just thinking about it. And then I think about him being in a helicopter and shooting and being shot at—I need to stop thinking about it—but I really can't!

Okay, so we did go to my brother's (that still sounds so weird) over Thanksgiving. It was strange and a little awkward at first, but it got better. Big John wasn't there, but Allen's wife, Sheila, knows sign language, so we all did just fine. Allen is really nice. He works at Gallaudet University in Washington, DC. I want to learn ASL (American Sign Language) so I can communicate better with him. We've written some to each other too.

Let's see, what else has been happening?

Pammy and I have been hanging out with Donna most of the time. We decided we are like The Three Musketeers. One of the guys in our friend group said we are more like The Three Stooges, but we vehemently opposed that suggestion. Vehemently is a word from a sentence that we had to diagram. I love diagramming sentences. Nouns, verbs, adjectives, and adverbs (which is what vehemently is.) Adverbs, words that describe verbs or adjectives. So many people say that all of that is so hard. Not to me. And not to Donna. It's a little hard for Pammy. Donna and I help her study for tests.

There are six of us who have lunch together, so we made up a club from our names. I told them I would only join if I could be Sue! There are three girls and three guys, and we use our middle names. "Rosie, Sue, Gail, Jeff, Gary, George." It's so stupid. We do crazy stuff during lunch like act out parts of movies. Jeff is so funny acting like one of the trees from "The Wizard of Oz" throwing apples. He cracks me up. I thought I knew Pammy through and through, but I never knew she could sound like Patty Duke's British cousin, Cathy. I'm probably the worst of all because all I ever do is sing something. At least I know lots of songs. We joke about doing a variety show sometime. Just not sure anyone else would be as entertained by us as much as we are by ourselves.

ENTRY DATE: Tuesday, March 5, 1968

Johnny left today for Viet Nam. He was able to go home for a week before leaving. He called me every night, but it didn't work out for him to come see me.

This is going to be the hardest thing I have ever been through. I am so worried about him. He said that in some ways he knows it's harder for others than for him. He gave me some Bible verses to read to help me.

John 3:16 again (God's love for the world)
Isaiah 41:10 (God's strength with us)
Proverbs 3:5–6 (trusting in God's plan)
Jeremiah 29:11 (God has a plan for our lives)
Philippians 4:6–7 (prayer and peace)
James 1:5 (asking God for wisdom)

It is so sweet of him to do that for me. I told him that Pammy and I still haven't gone to church yet, and he said it would be good to. I asked him if he goes to church and will it be hard to not be able to go in Viet Nam. He said he does go to church, and he'll still be able to go to church in Viet Nam. That's confusing to me because how do you have a church in a war zone??

Part 2: Summer 1967

ENTRY DATE: Friday, May 15, 1968

I've still been writing to Johnny every single day. I will keep all my letters from him in a special locked jewelry box that I got for Christmas.

School has gone by pretty quick. Pammy and Donna and I all decided to try out for cheerleading. It's pretty hard to make it because everybody that makes it is really popular—at least most are. But sometimes somebody will make it that hasn't already been a cheerleader for a couple of years. We'll see what happens. I think I'm pretty good. Better than some that were cheerleaders this year. I hope I make it so my senior year will be busy and fun. And will go by quickly.

I did get some great news from my parents. Since we now own the beach cottage we will be staying for a whole month. We've never done that before. Of course, Pammy will be coming as long as her parents say she can be gone that long. I sure hope so or else I wouldn't have anybody to hang out with since Johnny will be so very far away.

I live for days when I get a letter from him.

May 1, 1968

Hey Girl!

I got here safe. Sure hope I stay that way. This place can't even be described. SO DANG HOT!! I feel like I've sweated about ten pounds off already. I think my sweat is sweating.

Hopefully, I'll get used to it. Guess I don't have much choice, huh?

Sure hope you are doing well. Will you be going to the beach this summer? Think of me if you do. Probably the first thing I will do when I get back will be head to the beach. Right after I pick up my girl!

I keep your picture in my pocket all day long, and then at night I put it up on the bunk. It brings imagination to my mundane and calm to my chaos.

I don't have much to write about right now. Not sure what our first assignment will be. I should know in a day or two. One thing's for sure, I'm not in Kansas anymore! Or Philadelphia either! And for sure not Myrtle Beach!

All My Love,
Johnny

Part 3:
Summer 1968

Saturday, July 6, 1968

"The Times They Are a-Changin'"

This Diary Belongs to:

Rebekah Sue Lang

ENTRY DATE: Saturday, July 6, 1968

We're on our way to the beach right this very minute. The worst thing is I won't be home to get Johnny's letters for a WHOLE MONTH!! I brought the ones I already got with me. I will read them every day. It really makes me so sad for him to be there in such a terrible place. He signed the letter I just got with "All My Love!" Even those words sent flutters through my whole body. I miss him SO MUCH!!

And what he said about my picture was poetic . . . my heart!

Pammy was able to come, but the really weird thing is we'll be taking her to the next beach over for her to go to a cheerleading camp from June 17th to 21st and then picking her up after her camp. Yep, that's right!! Pammy made the cheerleading squad. And yep, that's right; I didn't. It helps to cushion the blow (which I think is the apropos expression) that

Donna didn't make it either. I had no idea that Pammy was so good. Everybody was asking her why she had never tried out before. She told me that she didn't tell them the reason, but it is because I never tried out before.

Well, at least I can say that I am best friends with one of the most popular girls. All cheerleaders are the most popular. I hope we stay best friends. Sometimes, being a cheerleader can change a girl. At least that's what I've heard.

This is our first beach vacation when I wasn't super excited with all kinds of ideas of what it will be like and what we will do. Even last year, I was determined to have the best time; I'm not even thinking about that this year.

Maybe that will be a good thing. A lot less disappointment for sure.

This is the first time I've seen Pammy sleep all the way to the beach. Maybe I should have invited Donna to come this year.

❦

Pammy and Rebekah *both* woke up just as the car pulled into the driveway of the little white cottage that now had a sign on a post that read "Auld LANG Sign," which had nothing to do with the beach. Rebekah always thought that part was mandatory. But it was what her father wanted because he thought it was clever. So what if they were one of those folks who had a sign that meant nothing to anyone but them?

Since they were seventeen—Pammy was closer to eighteen—perhaps they were just getting older, or perhaps the beach trips were getting old. Or perhaps neither was true, and they simply wanted to eat something first; whatever the reason, they both got out of the car and went straight to the kitchen without saying a word to each other. For the first time, they didn't jump out and run full speed toward the glorious strand.

Rebekah put the bag of groceries she carried on the table. The table, that just last summer had caused such angst—she had kept that word in her vocabulary since she hadn't been able to use it as much lately. With her whole life ahead of her, surely she would have opportunities galore to do just that. Especially with Johnny away at war. Life didn't get much more angst-filled than that!

"Pammy, have I ever fixed one of my famous peanut butter sandwiches for you?" Rebekah asked, knowing full well that she hadn't.

"I never knew you made a famous peanut butter sandwich." Pammy raised her brows. "What makes it famous . . . and who says it is?"

"Everyone who's ever had it says it is," Rebekah informed her, leaving out the fact that she, was the only person—that she knew of—who had actually had it. She offered it to her parents once, and they declined. Her father never ate peanut butter, which she had forgotten. How could anybody not like peanut butter? Her mother was "watching her weight" at the time of the offer and was not eating bread.

"You have to sit right there while I make it. Don't watch what I'm doing. It will be a surprise." Rebekah turned to the counter and began the process out of Pammy's sight.

Rebekah placed the paper plate with the sandwich, cut into triangles, in front of Pammy along with a glass of milk. She explained that serving milk with it made the whole thing a pièce de résistance.

"Where's yours?" Pammy asked, eyebrows raised.

"Oh, right here." Rebekah grabbed hers off the counter and sat across from Pammy. "Don't look inside it. The first bite will be a wonderful surprise, I promise."

Pammy waited for Rebekah to pick up a triangle before she lifted hers.

"So, what do you think? I'm right, right?" Rebekah asked while licking her lips.

"Mmm, it's different. Not bad. What is it, or can I look now?"

"Sure, go ahead and look." Rebekah took another big bite followed by a huge gulp of milk. "But drink some milk first."

Pammy peeled the slices of bread apart and peeked inside. "Cinnamon? Really? Cinnamon?"

"Yep," Rebekah exclaimed. "Isn't it so good? I discovered it a few weeks ago and can't stop eating them."

"It's not horrible. Not sure I'd eat it again and again. But it's definitely not horrible," Pammy surmised. "I'm surprised no one has ever thought of it before."

"Well, maybe somebody has, but I had never heard of it before, so I'm taking full credit for it. Maybe I'll even suggest it to diner owner. They can call it 'Sue's Peanut Butter Sandwich Surprise.' It's best to leave my real name off so that I don't end up losing my privacy once it becomes even more famous."

Rebekah laughed. It felt good to laugh. Maybe that's what they should concentrate on that week. Lots of good laughs. Now to figure out how to make that happen. She and Pammy never had to think about laughs before; they just happened. Wasn't that the secret to good laughs? Spontaneity?

The girls got ready for the beach as soon as they finished eating. Rebekah grabbed something from her suitcase and discreetly placed it in her beach bag.

"What was that?" asked Pammy.

"You'll find out soon; now let's get out of here." Rebekah brushed by Pammy, practically running out of the cottage.

༺ ༻

"Why"

Making their way to the oceanfront, Rebekah saw the notice stapled to a post. LIVE MUSIC ON THE BEACH in large print caught her eye.

"Well, I know what we're doing tomorrow night," she said, with enthusiasm that she hadn't felt in a long time.

"Wow. That's gonna be great. But it doesn't say who's gonna be playing," Pammy noted.

"Does it matter?" Rebekah asked.

As soon as they sat down on their beach towels, Rebekah glanced around, "Pretty sure it's safe to say we won't be tailed like a couple of criminals anymore."

She reached into her bag and pulled out the secret stash to show Pammy.

"W H A T are you doing with that?" Pammy swiveled her head from side to side, as if making sure no one watched them.

"You have three guesses. And the first two don't count," Rebekah answered.

Pammy rolled her eyes. "Okay, I'll rephrase my question . . . W H Y are you doing that?"

"Because I want to. It's no big deal. Haven't you thought about it? Almost every time I walk past the courtyard at school, I wonder what it would be like to be out there too," Rebekah held the cigarette between the fingers of her right hand and rifled through the bag again for the matches.

She turned toward Pammy and hunched over, away from the soft breeze. Even so, the first two matches were extinguished quickly. The third one stayed lit long enough for Rebekah to suck in deeply until the tip of the cigarette lit up. She held the smoke in for a few seconds before exhaling, looking and feeling very relaxed.

"I have so many questions right now. Like, how long have you been smoking? 'Cause you look like somebody in the movies, like some kind of professional cigarette smoker. Why are you even doing this? And most important: Why have you not told me? Do you have another friend that you smoke with? Do you and Donna smoke together—without me?"

By the time Pammy had finished her third-degree questioning, Rebekah had inhaled three or four more puffs, not once coughing or choking.

"Well, I almost told you a couple of times. I decided to wait until after cheerleading tryouts. Donna and I agreed that if either one of us made it, we would both quit smoking." Rebekah paused long enough to take in and exhale another drag. "Obviously, cheerleaders can't be smoking, and if only one of us made it, then the other one wouldn't want to smoke alone. And if we ended up quitting, there wouldn't be any reason to tell you."

Rebekah took one last long puff and put it out in the sand. She then pulled the cigarette pack out of the bag and placed the butt in it.

Pammy said nothing as she stood up, grabbed her things and walked away.

"Pammy, where are you going?" Rebekah called out.

"I'm leaving," Pammy answered, without turning around.

"Why?" Rebekah cocked her head.

Pammy paused. "If you have to ask me that, then I don't know what to tell you." Then off she went.

Rebekah shrugged her shoulders and watched her friend until she was out of sight.

Hmm. She didn't even give me a chance to offer her a puff of the next one.

"Help Me Rhonda"

Try as she may, Rebekah could not understand what Pammy was so upset about. She was all but one hundred percent sure that Pammy wouldn't have joined her and Donna anyway in such a "disgusting habit."

She'd talk to her, and they'd work it out. They always did.

But for the time being, she would lie there, soaking up the rays and smoking the cigs. She once heard somebody ask a store clerk if they had any Marlboro cigs, and she really liked the sound of that word—*cigs*—spoken with such confidence. Rebekah's personal "cig" choice was Tareyton. Her favorite for one very good reason—Eloise Lang had been unwittingly sharing them with her daughter. Rebekah could sneak a pack now and again without notice as long as it wasn't from a new carton. It worked out nicely for her that her mother hadn't quit smoking once her past life was no longer a secret. Yet Rebekah did ponder whether there were more secrets behind that decision to keep smoking.

Lighting another up, it occurred to Rebekah that she had quit sucking her thumb all those years ago, only to begin biting her nails; and she quit biting her nails only to incessantly pick at her cuticles. Maybe cigarette smoking would replace that habit. At least she didn't do all four. If anyone did do all four, they should definitely seek some therapy. Thankfully, she didn't need to.

Ah, yes, smoking relaxed her. Not completely, of course. Especially when it came to Johnny. She wondered how he was doing. What he was doing. Who he was with. What would he think of her smoking. Would he smoke with her?

She wondered how many letters would be awaiting her when she got home. She couldn't wait to open the ones she brought with her.

She suddenly remembered that she had told him she would write to him as soon as she got to the beach.

Rebekah finished her smoke, collected her things and headed to the small souvenir shop on the main strip.

The woman behind the cash register greeted her with such enthusiasm Rebekah supposed the woman thought she must know her. She turned to see if perhaps someone the woman did know had come in right behind her. No one had. In fact, it seemed that no one else at all was in the cluttered, overstocked shop.

The woman talked to Rebekah as if they had met. "How have you been, sweetie?" she asked, with a hint of a southern drawl.

"Good . . . thanks," Rebekah answered, as she closely examined the woman in hopes of sparking some memory of meeting her.

"Can I help you find anything in particular, or are you just lookin' to poke around some?"

"I'm looking for some postcards to send to someone very special, but I do want to look around first," Rebekah explained.

"Alrighty then, you just take your time, and I'll have those cards waiting right up here for you, sugar. Oh, and Rebekah, my name is Rhonda, if you need me for anything."

Oh, good grief. She knows my name. Who is she? Who is she?

Rebekah, racking her brain to remember the woman, hastily made her way down the aisle filled with seashells and glass figurines—mostly mermaids and turtles but also a few other lesser-known sea creatures.

She continued to the back of the shop where rows and rows of sun hats were displayed. An orange one just like the one her mother wore on the pier that day caught her eye. Well, that answered the question of where in the world she had gotten it.

The mirror, affixed to the back wall, was in perfect alignment with the check-out area. She could try on hats while sneaking peeks at Rhonda in hopes of triggering a memory. Twenty or so hats later, she still had nothing. She did, however, find a cute white and yellow one that would match her new white bikini. She was no Raquel Welch in it, but she was no Twiggy either. It was her new favorite. She made her way back to the front of the store to try on some sunglasses with the sun hat and to pick out postcards to send to Johnny.

"I Was a Fool"

Rebekah returned to the cottage, mulling over the encounter she had with the woman. She couldn't wait to tell Pammy everything, reminding herself that she first needed to make amends—again.

Pammy sat in the kitchen alone, her head resting on her folded arms.

"Hey, are you okay?" Rebekah asked.

Pammy lifted her head from the table. "Yeah, just really tired."

"Listen, that whole thing at the beach," Rebekah began, poking her head out of the kitchen doorway to be sure they were alone. "I should've explained it better. The reason I didn't say anything to you about the . . . you know . . . ," she continued in a low voice just in case one or both of her parents were hiding somewhere. Okay, they wouldn't be hiding. But it always felt like they were somewhere out of sight, eavesdropping. Especially when Rebekah was saying or doing something that they would consider devious.

"Well, because I didn't want you to think badly of me. And I figured you wouldn't want to do it now that you're a cheerleader, so I just kept it a secret. But I changed my mind. That's why I brought them to the beach. To share with you if you wanted to give it a try. So, do you?" Rebekah asked.

"Hmm, maybe. But please don't do that again. Whatever it is, just tell me. I want to be in on stuff, even if I decide not to do it, that doesn't mean I would stop being your friend or treat you any differently. You know that."

Rebekah nodded. "Okay, I promise. Let's go back down to the beach. I'll put together some sandwiches and chips to take. Donna said it's especially enjoyable right after a meal, so you can try your first one then. I've got so much to tell you; you won't even believe it."

While they ate their peanut butter and cinnamon sandwiches, sans the milk, since they didn't have a way to bring it to the beach with them, Rebekah reflected on her latest venture. As much as she prided herself in having just the right words, she was at a loss as to how to describe Rhonda. Would she say that Rhonda was strange? Or weird? Or odd? Those didn't seem to be the best words because she was really, really nice, and those words don't give that impression at all.

Before Rebekah had a chance to pull the cigarettes out of the bag, Pammy asked for one. "Just because it's best right after you eat doesn't mean you couldn't wait to at least swallow your last bite. Now that you're a cheerleader, you may want to think about the decision a little longer—to consider the possible repercussions."

"I get that. But you know what? I'm almost eighteen years old, and I haven't done anything wild or crazy. I haven't even kissed a boy. So, why shouldn't I smoke a cigarette if I want to?"

"You should. *If* you're sure you want to."

Pammy answered by grabbing the pack out of Rebekah's hand and digging for the matches herself. She lit one up, inhaled deeply, held it for a couple of seconds and blew the smoke out with her head slightly tilted upward. No coughing, spurting, or spitting. She even held it between her fingers and let it dangle there before taking a second puff—with the same sophistication as the first.

"Are you kidding me right now?" Rebekah asked indignantly. "I couldn't take a second puff until I tried again two days later. It was terrible. I almost threw up, I hacked and coughed so much—from just one little puff that I didn't even inhale. You can't tell me you've never done this before. I wouldn't believe you." Rebekah narrowed her eyes and pursed her lips.

Pammy let out the loudest and most annoying cackling laugh Rebekah had ever heard. On top of that, Pammy had no trouble taking a deep drag at the same time.

"You sound ridiculous. Why is that so funny?" Rebekah fumed.

"Oh, my gosh, Rebekah. I wish you could see your face right now. I really wish Donna could. It's exactly how we pictured you." Pammy kept laughing.

We? Rebekah almost got up to leave. But she didn't. That would only prolong the agony. The joke was on her, and she was determined to find out how and why Pammy—and apparently Donna—pulled this off. She crossed her arms and glared at her friend.

Pammy calmed down, took another drag. "I'm the one who got Donna to try it. Donna and I had lunch together, and we got to talking about needing to lose weight. So we decided to quit eating at lunch. After about a week of not eating, I told Donna that I read that smoking can help you lose weight too. You're not the only one who reads, Rebekah. We decided to try it together. The next day we just walked out to the back of the school and did it. Trust me, it took a few tries to get past the nastiness, but we did. And we've been doing it ever since. She supplies them and keeps us in stock as long as I pay for half, which I do. She also made me agree not to ask where she gets them, which I didn't—I don't."

"So why did you get so bent out of shape when I whipped them out?" Rebekah asked.

"I don't know, I just thought it would be fun to pull one over on you for a change."

Pammy glanced her way. "Except for the really good laugh, I guess it wasn't all that fun after all."

"I don't know what you mean by pull one over on me 'for a change,' but I'm not asking you to tell me either. My feelings have been hurt enough for one day. So, I say we sit here and enjoy our smokes and leave all that behind us, which, for the record is awfully big of me, wouldn't you agree?" Rebekah forced a small smile.

"I think that is incredibly big of you. So, what was it that you had to tell me?"

❧ ☙

"Never My Love"

"Okay, first of all, have you ever been in the little shop next to the Dairy Queen?" Rebekah asked.

"I've been in there a couple of times, why?"

"Well, today . . . I went today and the lady who works there, Rhonda, acted like she knew me, which confused the mess out of me because I couldn't remember ever meeting her or even seeing her before. But anyway, I went to the back of the store and found this sun hat." Rebekah touched her fingers to the brim of the hat as she turned to face Pammy.

"I like it, especially the yellow tie. Did they have any other colors?" Pammy asked.

"I don't know, probably. There's like a million of them. Remember the one my mother was wearing that day we saw her on the pier? I saw that one there. Anyway, so I go up to pay for it, and it's like she read my mind when she handed me this pair of yellow sunglasses that look perfect with it."

"I agree with Rhonda. They are perfect with that hat."

"Okay, but it's so strange that I was already thinking that I would love to find a pair of yellow sunglasses too. And there she was handing them to me. But, Pammy, that's not even the strangest part. While I'm standing there kinda dumbfounded, she hands me four postcards and says to me, 'I picked these out for you to send to Johnny. He's always talking about the amazing sunrises and sunsets. I know he'll love these.'"

"Huh? Who is this woman anyway?" Pammy's mouth twisted, and she opened her eyes wider.

"I know, right?" Rebekah shook her head. "Well, she went on to tell me that she's known Johnny since he was a little boy, and every summer he came in to buy saltwater taffy, a couple of Frisbees—always two because one inevitably ended up floating away—and two buckets with shovels for Robby and him. She said when he got older, he switched out the buckets and shovels for floats and kites."

Rebekah paused to light up another cigarette, handing that one and another to Pammy, who lit the second one with Rebekah's before returning it to her.

"Here's the clincher." Rebekah exhaled before continuing. "She said last summer, he told her about me. She said the way he described me, she knew it was me as soon as I walked in the door. While I was paying, she asked if he gave me the Bible? I asked how she knew about that, and she said he bought it in there last summer and told her it was for his girlfriend."

Rebekah's voice rose an octave or two. "That's me, Pammy. I'm his girlfriend. I think it is so cool that he told Rhonda that. But why didn't he tell me too? And I was wondering about that, standing there with her, but I didn't say it out loud. The next thing I know she looks at me, takes my hand and says that Johnny was so confused about how much he liked me and how hard it was knowing that he was leaving for the Army. She said he couldn't plan a future not knowing what lay ahead for him. But you know what I really don't understand? Why would she tell me all of that?"

They both sat quietly for a few minutes before Pammy spoke up. "Maybe she has some kind of magical powers, and she can see into the future. Like with the sunglasses. And somehow, she knows that Johnny's coming back and that you are going to get married, and she wants to be sure that you wait for him—maybe?"

"Wow, that totally makes sense. She doesn't know that I already decided that I'm waiting for him. Except if she can 'see' stuff, she should know that too," mused Rebekah.

"Well, whatever it is she knows or doesn't know, she sure knows Johnny. And Johnny must think an awful lot of her to tell her all about you, right?" Pammy asked.

Rebekah sighed, lay back on her beach towel, turned the radio on, and sang "Never My Love" along with The Association.

As soon as she got back to the cottage, she would get the first postcard ready to send to Johnny. He would know very soon what her song to him was. And he would know to go ahead and start planning their future together.

She surely was.

"Can't You Hear My Heartbeat?"

Rebekah was standing at the entrance, waiting for "The Best of the Beach" souvenir shop to open. She smiled at the teenage girl who approached the doorway with keys in hand.

"Good afternoon," the girl greeted her.

"Hello." She held out the postcard. I just wanted to bring this in time for the mail pickup. I wasn't sure when they came."

"Oh, sure, come on in. The mailman should be here around ten tomorrow morning." The girl opened the door and gestured for Rebekah to go first.

"I'm just really excited to get this in the mail." Rebekah set the postcard on the counter. "Is Rhonda coming back in today?"

"Rhonda? No, she hardly ever comes in anymore," the girl answered.

"Oh, I was in this morning, and she was very helpful. I was hoping to say hello to her." Rebekah glanced around the shop for her anyway.

"Huh? The shop was supposed to be closed until I just now opened it, so I don't know why she would have been here. I've worked here about a year, and I've never even seen her. She's owned this shop forever, but she hasn't worked here in years."

Rebekah placed the postcard in the mail pile on the counter and thanked the girl, wondering if Rhonda and Susan from the diner were some kind of mother and daughter disappearing act or something.

She decided to get some ice cream as soon as she stepped back out into the heat of the midafternoon sun. Even with her sunglasses on she squinted to see if it was Pammy in the short line of the Dairy Queen walk-up window. As she got closer, she could see that it was Pammy, but no amount of squinting helped her to recognize the girl she was chatting away with.

The girl was walking away by the time Rebekah approached Pammy. "What 'cha gettin?" she asked.

"Oh, hey. I think I'm gonna get some shaved ice. It's so dang hot right now." Pammy approached the window and ordered the pineapple flavor.

Rebekah thought about ordering a cup of just whipped cream but opted for a hot fudge sundae with nuts and extra-extra whipped cream instead. They headed toward the beachfront. By the time they reached the edge of the water, they had both finished their treats. They walked along silently for a while before Pammy spoke up.

"Did you see the girl I was talking to? She was telling me about tomorrow night and asking if I was coming down to the pavilion for the concert. I told her that me and my friend were coming. She said that's cool, and she would look for us."

"So, who is she?"

"I don't know, but she seems real nice."

"I'm so glad we have something to do tomorrow night. What should we do tonight though?" asked Rebekah.

"Won't we just do what we always do?" asked Pammy.

"Might as well." Rebekah resigned herself to going to the pavilion, but with none of the excitement and anticipation of the past. "I brought a book to read and some magazines to look at if you want to just go back and lie out on the beach for the rest of day."

Settled back down on their towels, Rebekah pulled a stack of magazines out of her bag. They each grabbed one and started flipping through the pages.

"Well, since I'm a cheerleader now, I guess I should check out the latest fashions, right?" Pammy asked.

Rebekah didn't bother to answer, somehow knowing that Pammy was basically asking herself the question. Probably joking since knowing what the latest fashions were was very different from owning and wearing any of them. And in that moment, a thought occurred to her that had never crossed her mind before.

She would talk to her mother first, but she had no doubt that her mother would be onboard with it. As excited as she was to share her great idea with Pammy, it would be way better to wait until school started up again in September. And this being their senior year would make the whole thing even better.

They both settled down on their tummies. Pammy to browse through *Seventeen Magazine*, and Rebekah to read *Romeo and Juliet*. She had started reading it when she and Mark started going steady, but she just couldn't get into it or understand Shakespeare's iambic pentameter—she learned of his writing style in last year's advanced literature course, that each of his lines contained a heartbeat.

Reading it now, with Johnny in mind, she completely understood how each line contained a heartbeat—just as true love should be.

"Twist and Shout"

Rebekah and Pammy were taking their time eating dinner before going back out. Her mother had made meatloaf, baked potatoes, and corn-on-the-cob. Very little conversation took place as they enjoyed each bite.

Rebekah was forced to speak up, though, when her father started reaching for a second serving of the "World's Best Meatloaf"—so named by Pammy the first time she had it. Of course, in her estimation, everything that Eloise Lang made was the "World's Best."

"Daddy, we have to leave enough for meatloaf sandwiches tomorrow," she chastised him.

"There's plenty. Your mother made two just for that reason," he assured her.

Without looking up from her plate, Pammy posed a question to Rebekah. "Are they as good as your famous peanut butter surprise sandwich?"

Rebekah, well aware that her friend was being facetious, shot back at her in the same manner. "That's a lot to ask. I know my mother is an amazing cook and this meatloaf is stupendous in its mouth-watering flavor, but it's unfair of you, or anyone for that matter, to expect it to be compared to my one-of-a-kind gourmet sandwich."

Sharing a good laugh around the table, Rebekah realized laughter had been dearly missing for far too long.

As soon as they finished eating, the girls cleared the table and chattered back and forth about the next night's live music event. They named one song after another that they hoped to hear them play, even though they knew nothing about them or the kind of music they played. But they had to agree that they were sure to love it because it was live music at the beach and although they had never actually heard live music at the beach, it had to be as good as it got.

Heading up to the pavilion fifteen minutes later, they were met with of a downpour that lasted just long enough to drench them from head to toe before ending as abruptly as it began.

It was a warm and muggy evening, made more so by the short rain event. Neither Rebekah nor Pammy expressed concern with going back to change. They continued on their way as if soaking wet hair, clingy clothes, and soggy sneakers were the latest fashion trend. Besides, neither of them hoped to meet—or even thought about boys at all. That had to be a first. What possible difference could it make if they waited however long it took to dry out?

The Beach Boys' "Surf City" filled the air as they made their way into the crowded space and meandered through the many dry-haired and properly dressed kids to find a table that had just been vacated by a couple of hippie-looking guys.

There were just a few kids back at school who fit the hippie description, but they didn't know them. Everyone pretty much left them alone. They were basically considered to be freaks who were probably smoking marijuana and protesting the Viet Nam war every chance they got. The girls had never been around marijuana, but they had heard about it plenty. Just reading about how it smelled was enough to shut down any possible interest. On second thought, hadn't Rebekah felt the same way about smoking cigarettes not so long ago?

Starting to feel somewhat uncomfortable in her wet clothes, Rebekah was reminded of another time when they were soaked to the bone.

"Remember the last time we got soaked like this?" She sat at the table. Before Pammy could answer, two boys slid into the vacant seats. They must have been hovering close by, waiting for the first chance to hit on some girls. Rebekah thought they must be desperate to pick two girls who looked like they'd just come in from a moonlight swim.

"Hey, there," one of them said, in a creepy voice, before he had even completely settled in the seat next to Pammy. Clearly, he had never been told how important first impressions were.

Once the other boy took his seat next to Rebekah, the boy next to Pammy posed a question, looking from one girl to the other. "So, which one you dolls wants to dance with me?"

Rebekah rolled her eyes at Pammy expecting to burst into uncontrollable laughter together. But without even cracking a smile Pammy stood up. "I do." And off they went hand-in-hand to the dance floor to "Twist and Shout" with The Beatles and a dance floor full of happy-go-lucky vacationers.

Content to sit through one of her most favorite songs, Rebekah sang along, only to be interrupted by the boy next to her. He seemed nervous, not at all like his cocky counterpart, when he shyly asked if she'd like to dance too.

"Not really," she answered, certain that he would say a quick goodbye—or not—and leave to find another desperate looking girl. He didn't go anywhere though. He sat right there, although he did turn slightly to watch the action on the dance floor.

Rebekah thought about all the times she and Pammy had danced in her living room, almost always when her parents were gone. They would turn up the music loud enough for the bass to reverberate through the floor and walls, but not so loud that the neighbors would complain. Thankfully, there was plenty of room between their house and the ones on each side. Even better was the sound barrier provided by the row of huge azaleas that had been planted before Rebekah was born. And a fair share of tall pines and white and pink dogwoods.

Watching Pammy twisting, turning, and shouting, she was convinced that all their private dance parties had paid off. She didn't think she'd seen Pammy have so much fun before. At least not in a really long time. At the same time, it made her miss Johnny more than ever. One day she and Johnny would dance the night away. One day.

Until then, she would watch and listen. And sing.

"I'm Only Sleeping"

"I can't believe I had my first kiss tonight," Pammy sighed, as the two of them settled in for the night. "I guess it's time for me to get a diary too, huh?"

It had been a very long day, and Rebekah was just too tired to think about her horribly boring night of sitting for hours with the horribly boring boy, whose name she did not bother to find out. She lost interest in having even a casual conversation as soon as he told her he wasn't really much into music. She figured he must not really be much into girls either, since he seemed perfectly content to sit with one who clearly was not at all interested in him.

She found solace in the fact that for her—and any other normal person—time spent with music was never wasted, thus she was somewhat content to watch Pammy and Mr. Obnoxious dance the night away.

She only stayed to keep an eye on Pammy. As long as they were dancing, she knew the smooth talker was harmless. But he had the nerve to come over to her when Pammy went to the bathroom to ask if she was jealous and, if so, there was plenty of him to go around. She intended to grab Pammy as soon as she came back and insist they get out of there.

When Pammy did come back though, she was practically radiating with pure happiness, and Rebekah didn't have the heart to out him to her. She gave him an "I'm watching you and you better not hurt my friend or else" look that seemed to be enough to knock his cockiness down a notch or two.

The bed, her pillow, Johnny's picture, and Ralphie were exactly what Rebekah needed to fall into a much-anticipated deep sleep—and hopefully to dream about Johnny. She wondered if he had dreamed about her yet.

Pammy continued to chatter away. "I know you're really tired, and I know you think Kevin is . . . I don't know what you think he is . . . but I can tell you don't like him. But oh, my gosh, I had so much fun. He is super nice to me, and I can't wait to see him again tomorrow. I'll stop talking and let you get to sleep now."

Rebekah was so close to falling asleep, she didn't bother answering.

She awoke early the next morning with no memory of Johnny dreams, or any dreams at all for that matter. She hadn't remembered any dreams for a long time. No dreams were way better than the insane ones she'd been known to have.

"Do you have any aspirin?" Pammy asked, groggily, as she tried to wake up.

"There's some in the medicine cabinet. I'm going to the bathroom. I'll get you some," Rebekah answered.

Although this was the first time Pammy had asked for aspirin at the beach, Rebekah recalled that she had been taking a lot of aspirin over the past few weeks. She grabbed the bottle and headed to the kitchen for water and a quick look in the fridge for lunch ideas.

She wanted to spend the whole day tanning, so she had planned to pack a bunch of food and drinks. There it was, just as her father promised, a whole meatloaf just waiting to be sliced and slapped between two thick pieces of homemade sourdough bread—each slathered with a thick layer of Duke's mayonnaise. Her mother had gotten some other brand once, but she never made that mistake again, after the full jar sat in the fridge so long it expired.

Rebekah had placed everything for the sandwiches on the counter when she heard something strange. She followed the sound to the closed bathroom door where she heard retching and within a few seconds, water running. She turned quickly back to the bedroom where Pammy followed in turn.

"Was that you?" Rebekah asked Pammy.

"Yeah, I get sick sometimes when I have a really bad headache," she explained.

"Here's the aspirin." Rebekah handed them to Pammy and returned to the kitchen for the water. She was getting worried that a whole day of tanning might not happen after all. Although, even if Pammy wasn't feeling well, she, herself, should probably still go. It wasn't like she could help her with anything. Maybe Pammy just needed to sleep some more.

Pammy followed her to the kitchen. "I feel a little better. I usually do after I throw up, for some reason."

Then, as if she had read Rebekah's mind, she said, "I'm not staying in all day that's for sure."

"Come on, let's get all our food together and get out of here." Rebekah turned around to get their "gourmet" sandwiches ready.

Sunday, July 7, 1968

"Cherish"

Two songs had already played all the way through when Rebekah shot up from her prone position and asked loudly, "You got your first kiss? Did you tell me that last night?"

Pammy had popped straight up before Rebekah finished her questions. She frantically scanned from side to side to see what had caused the sudden outburst. "Good grief, you scared the mess out of me." Pammy held her right hand to her chest as she slapped Rebekah's right arm with her other one.

"Did you tell me that?" Rebekah repeated her question.

"Yes, you know I did. It's not that big of a deal."

"Not a big deal? It's your first kiss . . . I was right there . . . how did I not see it?" Rebekah was flabbergasted by that very important and disturbing detail. She had been watching him like a hawk and yet, somehow, he slipped one in, anyway.

"Why would you care about seeing my first kiss? I think that's kinda creepy." Pammy's nose crinkled as she stared at Rebekah.

"What song was playing?" Rebekah ignored Pammy's concern.

"Why?"

"It's important for me to know."

"'Cherish' . . . by The Association," Pammy said, smiling as she said the word *cherish*. "We started slow dancing, and just like that, he kissed me. It was magical. I've never had a favorite song before. But I do now, and it will be my favorite song for the rest of my life," Pammy spoke so softly that Rebekah barely heard her.

That explained it. As soon as the song started, Rebekah had closed her eyes. She had kept them closed through the entire song, imagining Johnny singing it to her. And she kept them shut for a few seconds after it ended. By the time she opened them again, Pammy and Kevin were doing "The Loco-Motion" with Little Eva, and the other dancers scattered around the dance floor.

"Just one kiss then, right?" Rebekah asked.

"Just one . . . Why are you so interested in this?" Pammy lay back down, turning her head away from Rebekah. "I don't want to talk it about anymore."

Rebekah wasn't ready to let it go. "I just don't want to see you jumping into something just so you can say that you have kissed a guy. You don't really know him at all, Pammy."

Pammy shot up again. "You don't get to place rules on how or why

I do anything, Rebekah! Who's the one whose first kiss was with a boy she really didn't know? Who's the one who lied to him about her age? You know I could go on and on and on, so . . . No, you don't get to do this. Just leave me alone."

As much as it stung, Rebekah knew Pammy was absolutely right. But Pammy didn't know what she knew. That Kevin was a jerk. No girl's first kiss should be with a jerk. But the damage was done, and nothing was gonna change it. And the only way for Pammy to understand why Rebekah was saying all this would be to enlighten her—that her very first kiss ever was with a jerk—and no girl needed to hear that, especially from her best friend.

"Can't wait for the band on the beach tonight," Rebekah said, hoping that changing the subject to something less provocative would lighten the mood. Provocative…yet another word she'd recently come across, assuming once again it wouldn't fit in her life any time soon.

How many times had she been wrong when she wondered if, how, or when—this, that, or the other—would be relatable to her past, present, or future? Too many to count for sure. Maybe one day she would live each day as it came and stop overthinking everything. Maybe.

Since Pammy didn't answer, Rebekah lay back, took a deep breath, and started humming "Cherish."

She fell asleep just after reaching over to turn the radio on.

"Hold On, I'm Comin'"

Rebekah woke up to and joined The 5th Dimension singing "Up, Up and Away," immediately followed by The Beatles' "Penny Lane" and "With a Little Help from My Friends." Finishing that last one, she looked over to see that her friend was no longer there. She sat up and looked around, but she figured Pammy must have left a good while ago. There was no sign of her anywhere.

She lit one of the three cigarettes she confiscated from the pack her mother had left on the kitchen table. As soon as she took the last drag, she put it out, crammed it into the bag, collected her things, and headed to the pavilion.

Damage control. Again.

Finding the pavilion almost empty was not unusual at that time of day. Even the regulars didn't get there until early afternoon, and it was barely eleven. She scanned the area for Pammy but spotted someone else.

"Hello, Rhonda," she said as she tapped the woman on the shoulder.

Rhonda spun around. Her face lit up as she gave Rebekah a hug that one might expect to receive if they'd been found after being missing for so long that everyone had given up any hope of finding them alive.

"Hey there, sugar." She rubbed Rebekah's arm.

Rebekah stopped just before asking Rhonda what she was doing there, realizing it would make no sense to question someone she didn't really know, who lived and owned a business there, as to why she would be anywhere. Just because Rebekah—for no good reason—was surprised to see her.

"Are you having a good time?" Rhonda asked in such a genuine way that it seemed as though she was sincerely hoping for an adamant yes.

Not wanting to disappoint her, Rebekah managed a somewhat convincing nod. "I was just looking for my friend. I don't see her though, so she might have gone back to the cottage. I'm sure I'll find her."

Rebekah turned to leave when Rhonda called out to her. "I just saw a pretty young girl with short black hair walking on the beach with that real nice boy, Kevin. Is that maybe your friend?"

"What? You know Kevin?" Rebekah was stunned. There was no way that was the same Kevin. But she still turned around, walked across the wood floor to the steps leading out to the beach, just in case he was indeed the same Kevin. Kevin, who had apparently pulled the wool over Rhonda's eyes. Could she possibly have known him as long as she'd known Johnny? Rebekah had just met him, and she already knew he was not as Rhonda believed.

Rebekah rushed across the sand. The knot in her gut and voices in her head urged her on. She had to protect Pammy. Pammy was naive and way too trusting. And not a very good judge of character. Obviously.

Perhaps guilt motivated her most. She just had to find them. She should have been more proactive in helping Pammy find a boyfriend. A nice guy. A good guy. One like Johnny. Then Pammy wouldn't be so desperate. She had been so obsessed with her own love life that she had all but ignored poor Pammy's lonely heart. Pammy had been such an amazing matchmaker with her and Johnny, going above and beyond to make sure they got together and stayed that way.

She would find Pammy and save her from the biggest mistake of her life, and that would make up for the many times she had let her best friend down.

Whatever scenes she had conjured up in her imagination did not prepare her for what played out in reality several yards from her. She had briefly glanced toward the sand dunes to her left, only to jerk her head back in that direction once her brain processed what her eyes already had.

There was Pammy lying helpless with that horrible, fake, creepy, obnoxious brute over top of her.

Rebekah felt like she was running in slow motion while also gaining a strength that defied the natural ability to do exactly what she intended to do. She pushed Kevin off Pammy with such force that he rolled all the way over to another sand dune. He yelped and lay still.

Rebekah reeled from the surge of adrenaline as she tried to nudge Pammy back to a conscious state. Once Pammy did come to, she sat up and screamed for Kevin.

"Oh, my God, are you okay? Did I get to you in time? Did he hurt you, Pammy?" Rebekah glanced over at Kevin to be sure that he was still lying there. He was.

"What are you talking about?" Pammy asked, rubbing her head. "Where's Kevin?"

"You don't have to worry about him now. He's not coming anywhere near you as long as I have anything to do with it."

By this time, several beach-goers had gathered around, most of them with Pammy and Rebekah and a few with Kevin, checking on him and offering help. One woman had run to get a lifeguard.

Why were they asking him if he was okay?

The lifeguard appeared within minutes with the first aid kit.

And with something else as well.

"So Wrong"

While the lifeguard checked on Kevin, the police officer squatted in front of the girls.

"You want to tell me what happened here?" he inquired.

Rebekah shook from the adrenaline that was slowly leaving her body. "This is my friend, Pammy, and . . . and . . . and that boy viciously attacked her," she screeched.

Pammy's mouth dropped open.

Before the officer could continue, Rebekah elaborated, "I got here in time to push him off her, or who knows what he would have done. I knew as soon as I met him that he was trouble, but I never thought he was capable of this kind of heinous behavior." *Heinous* was yet another word she'd fallen in love with, never thinking she would use it so soon after learning it.

The officer held Rebekah's gaze. "So, you witnessed the whole thing, ma'am?"

"Well . . . no . . . not exactly. Like I said, I got here in time to stop it. Just in time to push him off her—like I said." The blood coursed through Rebekah's veins. It's like they were in their very own real-life crime story. And she was the star!

She loved watching crime shows and understood the importance of keeping one's story straight. Of course, if someone told the truth, they didn't have to worry about that.

Dragnet was her favorite as far as the drama of it all, but her absolute favorite was *77 Sunset Strip*. Because of Kookie, of course. He was dreamy. There were other cop shows she really liked, but those two were, by far, her absolute favorites.

"Okay. Thank you for that. I'd like to talk to your friend now. So, if you can just step back—not where the young man is—on the other side." He motioned to his left where the others had stood before he asked everyone who wasn't involved to leave. Rebekah took a few steps in that direction, still facing Pammy.

The officer motioned for her to step farther away, which she did. Watching the crime shows also taught her to do exactly as you were told—if you wanted to make your life a lot easier. She had hoped to hear the officer's questions or Pammy's responses but was unable to, so she turned her attention to Kevin.

Although she couldn't hear what was being said there either, she could see that the lifeguard had called for additional help. From what she could tell, Kevin seemed to be pretty badly hurt. Blood covered his shirt and abdomen, causing a slew of mixed emotions to rush over her.

Rebekah was completely justified in feeling proud of herself for bravely protecting her friend, but she didn't particularly feel like celebrating the fact that she caused someone such distress. Even if the someone was one of poor character who had maliciously attacked her friend. The justification did not ease the sorrow. What had she done? She had never deliberately hurt someone before. Not physically anyway.

She plopped herself down on the ground, burying her head between her knees, and sobbed quietly. Why did it feel so wrong to do the right thing?

She thought of Johnny and whether he might be dealing with the same conflicting emotions—on a much bigger scale, of course.

Or was war a realm of its own—where mixed emotions were necessarily replaced by no emotions at all?

"Easier Said Than Done"

The officer had asked Pammy to stay put and motioned to Rebekah to do the same. He made his way over to Kevin, where the medic was applying a large bandage to his wound. The officer spoke to Kevin for just a few minutes and then told the girls to come over to where he and Kevin were. Kevin sat up.

"After speaking to all three of you, I have ascertained that a misunderstanding led to this unfortunate incident."

Rebekah opened her mouth in protest, but the officer gave her a stern look that said, "Be quiet." She got the message loud and clear.

He continued to speak, without interruption, repeating each of their stories back to them, starting with Rebekah's. He graciously explained that she was under the impression that the young man was hurting her friend and acted accordingly.

He then related Pammy's story, that while she and Kevin walked on the beach, she began to feel faint and, according to her, the young man carried her up to the dunes in an effort to shield her from the direct sunlight. That was all that she remembered before she did, in fact, faint.

The officer continued by saying that Kevin gave the same version of the event Pammy did but added that as he was leaning over her to be sure she was breathing, he was knocked over by an unknown force, causing him to land on a reed that penetrated his abdomen.

The officer looked at each of them. "Does anyone have anything to add to these statements?"

When no one spoke, the officer focused his gaze on Rebekah. "Kevin is going to be fine. He said he won't seek any retribution for his injury, as he understands why you wanted to protect your friend."

Rebekah was mortified. Heat scorched her cheeks.

Her first instinct had been that Kevin would lie. But having time to sit a while and to replay the whole thing as the officer described it, she realized she'd been completely wrong.

She looked at Pammy and then Kevin, and said, "I'm so sorry. I guess I allowed my imagination to go a little wild."

Kevin offered a gentle smile that told her he held no grudge.

Rebekah received no such assurance from her friend. Perhaps she had crossed a line this time. She would not be able to smooth this over with a simple, albeit sincere, apology.

She messed up. She messed up real bad, and she knew it.

❦ ❧

"All You Need is Love"

Rebekah had tried several times to talk to Pammy about it. All that Pammy said was that she didn't want to talk about anything at all. And she hadn't. Rebekah's few attempts at reversing her friend's decision were met with no response.

They had gotten ready to go to the "Live Music On The Beach" concert in silence. As sad as it made her, she decided to just leave Pammy alone. And as tempting as it was to tell her why she believed Kevin might hurt her, she knew Pammy was too upset right now and wouldn't listen to anything Rebekah had to say. She would probably think that Rebekah made it all up.

At least they would still walk up there together to do something that would brighten both of their moods. Live music on the beach—she could hardly believe their luck.

By the time Rebekah and Pammy reached the area where the make-shift stage had been built, the group—whose name remained a mystery—was warming up as the stagehands set up microphones and speakers. Rebekah had never been to a live music event before and just witnessing the preparation caused her excitement to skyrocket. She was already moving to the music as it was, as she took in the scene before her.

She recognized the two hippy-looking guys she'd seen at the pavilion, and she thought she recognized the girl Pammy had talked to in the Dairy Queen line. She noticed something odd about the girl that she hadn't noticed before as they all bustled around crazily getting instruments tuned and such.

She turned to ask Pammy if it was indeed the same girl, but Pammy was no longer standing with her. A quick scan of the fast-growing crowd was unsuccessful in sighting her. She wasn't sure Pammy would have answered her anyway. How long could Pammy hold out? Who else was she going to talk to? Oh, yeah, Kevin. Rebekah still wanted to get to the absolute truth about him. She knew that she knew that he said what he said to her. But she also knew that she knew that he was very forgiving toward her on the beach earlier.

So, there she stood, the one with nobody to talk to.

But not for long. Another quick scan made visible someone who was becoming a regular in her life. She made her way toward her, still moving her hips and shoulders to the music tune-ups.

Rhonda spotted her before Rebekah could call out to her. Running to her with open arms, Rhonda's radiant smile was like a magnet. Rebekah was filled with warmth and affection at the sight of her. Maybe her endearing feelings had everything to do with the fact that Rhonda knew Johnny so well. Possibly better than Rebekah even did. Rhonda cared for the person that she, herself, cared for more than anyone else in her life. They had something really important in common. She was beginning to believe she had found a friend for life in Rhonda.

"Hey there, sweetie," Rhonda yelled over the non-harmonious sounds of guitar, drum, and keyboard tune-ups. "Did you find your friend?"

Rebekah nodded her head in affirmation but had no interest in elaborating.

If Rhonda had any intentions of asking further questions, she was cut off by the group leader speaking to the crowd.

The bright blue and orange bandana kept his long brown hair away from his face. His was the first beard Rebekah had seen on someone younger than Santa Claus. He wore blue jeans and a white short-sleeved undershirt. He wore no shoes. In fact, they were all barefoot.

"Hello, Myrtle Beach," he called out with excitement and enthusiasm.

In return, the diverse crowd greeted him with cheers. Rebekah, still hoping to spot Pammy, was quite surprised to see folks of all ages. Families and people old enough to be her parents and even grandparents were scattered among the many teens.

"All right, thanks for coming out tonight. Are you ready to rock?"

Again, the crowd let out a resounding affirmation.

"We're gonna start off with some of *our* favorite songs. I'm pretty sure they're some of *your* favorites too. So please feel free to sing along. The best songs are meant to be sung loudly by all, right?"

Rebekah now knew that the girl making her way to one of the mics was indeed the girl she had seen at the Dairy Queen. The girl placed the palm of her left hand around the microphone cartridge and lowered it close to her mouth—Rebekah had recently seen a diagram of one with the parts labeled. She often wondered why things were named the way they were. Why not just call it the handle or the stem?

She also often wondered why she wondered about so much. Case in point, she wondered why three of the girl's fingers were missing just above the knuckles. To her complete amazement, the girl began strumming the guitar with the two remaining fingers and the tips of the three. Rebekah knew little to nothing about playing instruments, but seeing this girl's whole fingers working together with the shorter ones mesmerized her. She was a wonder to behold. The girl's long, straight blonde hair, tossed to and fro by the evening breeze, seemed to be moving with the increasingly louder music.

Several notes in and Rebekah excitedly clapped with anticipation. She began singing along from the first word of "All You Need Is Love," one of her most absolute favorite Beatles' songs ever. To her sheer delight, the group—whose name had yet to be mentioned—without the slightest pause, started right in with another of her most absolute favorite Beatles' songs, "Can't Buy Me Love."

It was as if they had asked her to pick the songs for the night. Rebekah had never experienced such musical bliss, as they sang one Beatles song after another. "Love Me Do," "P. S. I Love You," and "You've Got to Hide Your Love Away" stirred the crowd, mostly the teens, into a delightful frenzy. It made no difference at all that one of the four in the unnamed group was a girl, or that not one of them wore those cute "John Lennon" glasses. Never mind that none of them looked anything at all like Paul, John, George, or Ringo. Or that they couldn't possibly measure up to the Beatles. As far as Rebekah was concerned, the Beatles themselves may as well have been performing right there in front of her. Of course, it was best that Paul McCartney wasn't there in person. She most surely would have embarrassed herself. It was a sure bet she wouldn't have been the only one.

After the final note of the fifth song, the lead singer introduced himself and the rest of the group members, garnering several rounds of applause. He told them that the four of them were local residents who had played together for about a year. He said that, although they all had individual names, they did not have a group name because they didn't want one because they had no intention of becoming well-known. *How odd*, Rebekah thought. Who wouldn't want to be well-known if they could?

He went on to say that they would play more songs, but he had a question to pose to the listeners. "Did anyone pick up on a theme?"

Several folks yelled out, "The Beatles."

Rebekah was sure he was looking for another less obvious answer. As loud as she could she shouted, "Love."

The young man, who had introduced himself as Mitch, heard hers over the other guesses, "Who just said 'love'?"

Rhonda grabbed Rebekah's arm and pulled it as high as she could, practically pulling her off the ground. Mitch pointed at her. "Yes! What's your name?"

"Rebekah," she called out.

"You got it, Rebekah. We're talking love out here tonight. So, let's keep going, what do ya say?"

The group started up again in response to the thundering applause.

Three more Beatles songs, "She Loves You," "And I Love Her," and "Love Me Do" rounded out the first half of the performance, and then Mitch told the crowd to hang around while they took a short break.

Quite a few took seats on the cooling sand. Some remained standing. No one left.

Rebekah had been so caught up in the musical extravaganza that she hadn't thought of Pammy since the music started. Now that things had calmed down, she turned to Rhonda. "Have you seen Kevin here tonight?"

Rhonda shook her head. "Sure haven't, sweetie."

She contemplated, but decided against, also asking how Rhonda knew Kevin. That question alone could lead to more Kevin-talk than Rebekah was interested in.

"Are You Lonesome Tonight?"

Still no sign of Pammy . . . Rebekah started getting somewhat nervous. If not for the whole debacle earlier in the day, she probably would have made her way in and through the crowd in a desperate search for her friend. But now, that would only add to her friend's ire.

She convinced herself that Pammy and, possibly—probably—Kevin were somewhere in the mix waiting for the group to return as was everyone else. She turned to talk some more with Rhonda while quiet prevailed.

But Rhonda was nowhere to be seen. Rebekah began to get a little paranoid. And a lot lonely.

Thankfully, the band returned, and, after a short warm-up, Mitch called out to everyone once again.

"So, who's ready for some more music? We're gonna switch it up a bit, okay?"

The crowd cheered as the group began another set, starting with Elvis's "Can't Help Falling in Love." Rebekah had hoped and expected it to be a full night of The Beatles, but as long as they stuck with them and Elvis, they had her full attention.

They played "Don't Be Cruel" next. Mitch wasn't half-bad in his Elvis impression. Pretty entertaining, actually. Hard as she tried, though, she could not picture Elvis wearing long hair held back with a bright bandana. She laughed out loud at the thought.

It sure seemed as though they had been at this for more than a year. Maybe she hadn't heard correctly. Granted, Rebekah had never been to a live concert before, but she couldn't imagine it being much better—unless, of course, Elvis was there *with* The Beatles. That would be crazy. She wondered if they had ever done a concert together. Probably not. The local radio station did a call-in contest to vote for who was the best, Elvis or The Beatles. It made it seem like they were rivals who probably didn't like each other much. But she probably made that up in her mind.

Mitch interacted with a few folks, and then each of the band members played solo for a while before continuing with Elvis's "It's Now or Never," "Love Me Tender," and "Return to Sender."

Rebekah thought of hers and Johnny's letters and how heartbroken she would be if any of her letters were returned with "address unknown" or "no such number" or "no such zone." She wished she could get on a plane right then, that minute, and fly all the way to Viet Nam to be with him. How was she ever going to get through this? How was Johnny going to?

Was Johnny going to?

The group kicked up the pace with "Blue Suede Shoes" and "Hound Dog." Mitch then asked everyone to stick around for a few minutes after the last song because he had something super cool to tell them.

They finished the night of "Live Music on the Beach" by saying that if anyone wanted to ask someone to dance, this was the time to do so.

Rebekah finally caught a glimpse of Pammy and Kevin. Apparently, they had been standing directly in front of the stage the entire night. They and tons of others took Mitch's suggestion and moved close together.

Rebekah stared at her friend and sang every single word of "Are You Lonesome Tonight?" with a heavy heart that somehow did not physically break in two. There was no point or desire in trying to hold anything back. Her fingers linked and cupped together in front of her chin, caught each tear that fell steadily from her wet cheeks.

൞൸

"Soul Man"

Although Rebekah had intended to stick around to hear what else Mitch had to say, she just couldn't do it. Not after that song.

But as she began making her way toward the pavilion to cross through on her way back to the cottage, she could still hear him. His words got her full attention. She turned around at the steps to listen.

"Thanks everybody for coming out. We sure do hope you enjoyed yourselves as much as we did. If you don't mind hangin' out for just a few more minutes, I'd like to share a little something with y'all."

Only a few folks made their way off the beach. Almost everyone's curiosity had been piqued.

"I can tell that this crowd loves The Beatles as much as we do."

The crowd clapped and cheered in agreement.

"Let me ask you something. This is kinda weird, but have any of you heard the rumor about what John Lennon said about the popularity of The Beatles?"

A couple of folks raised their hands, but most just shook their heads.

"Well, John Lennon said something about how The Beatles were more popular than Jesus. And before you think about getting indignant—like I did when I first heard that—just let me give a little different perspective. He ain't wrong. You heard me right—John Lennon ain't wrong."

The crowd became so quiet that if not for the brilliance of the full moon, Rebekah wouldn't know for sure that they were still there.

Mitch continued. "You see, the sad truth is that The Beatles probably are more popular than Jesus. Maybe that's because we don't talk enough about this man, Jesus. Who he was, and who he is. When we get to know him—and crazy as that sounds—we can get to know him, then he becomes the most important person in our lives. You see, The Beatles can and do entertain us, and we can appreciate their talent. But The Beatles, while they just may be more popular than Jesus, they cannot save us from our sins. Only Jesus, God's only Son, can do that."

Some of the crowd started leaving after the second mention of the name, Jesus. Several more after the third and fourth mention.

Quite a few had left by the time Mitch asked another question.

"What's Elvis's nickname?"

Pretty much everyone who was still there yelled out, "The king of rock and roll."

"Yep, that's right, or just The King. And you know what? He probably is the king of rock and roll. But for sure he ain't . . . *The King*. The Bible tells us that Jesus Christ is the King of kings, the Lord of lords, and the Prince of Peace. And He loves you, every single one of you. It don't matter what you've done, where you've been, or nothin' else. There ain't nothin' any of us can do to lose His love. That love cost Him His life. A life that he gave freely for us, so we too can have eternal life. And you know what? It's free. Free for the believin'.

"We're gonna be hangin' around here as long as anyone wants to talk some more about this King, this Savior, and how to know Him . . . So come on up, and let's talk." Mitch smiled and waved to everyone to come on down.

"We love y'all. It's been a blast hangin' out together," he finished as he walked away from the mic.

Rebekah sat down on one of the steps to contemplate all that Mitch said. As she sat there, she noticed that Pammy, Kevin, and about ten to fifteen other kids were still down by the stage talking to Mitch and the other band members.

All Rebekah could think about was getting to her diary. She had so much to "talk" about.

☙❧

"Do You Want to Know a Secret"

With the pillow against the headboard, and her back against the pillow, Rebekah brought her knees up to prop her diary. She had no sooner written the date when Pammy entered the bedroom. Pammy allowed no time for Rebekah to say the words that were ready to spew at the sight of her friend. Words that may have been harsh only because her brain was about to burst with everything she wanted—needed—to relieve it of.

"I wish you had stayed to hear what Mitch said after the concert," Pammy's voice shook. She seemed to have completely forgotten that she didn't want to talk to Rebekah.

"I just needed to get back to write some stuff down." Rebekah hoped that Pammy would take the hint and find someone else to "preach" to.

"He was telling us about how Jesus came all that long time ago to forgive us for our sins," Pammy said. She had not taken Rebekah's hint.

Rebekah was a little curious, enough to clarify exactly what sins he was referring to. "You mean, like smoking?"

"He told us that God is righteous, and all of us and everybody who has ever lived or will live have sinned because we all rebel against God. And we don't love Him. But He still loves us and wants us to be with Him forever. But we can't be because only righteous people can be in Heaven." Pammy took a deep breath. "You should talk to Mitch. He can explain it better than me."

Rebekah actually kinda understood what she was saying. Kinda.

"Anyway, because God loves us so much, He sent His Son, Jesus, to live on earth. And because Jesus lived a sinless life, He was the only one who could save us from our sins. He died on a cross for the punishment of all our sins." Pammy seemed to have exhausted her knowledge of this newly acquired information, prompting Rebekah to do what she had wanted to do before Pammy's rant.

"Okay, Pammy; that's a whole lot to take in, and I already had a ton of stuff to write about, so would you mind going somewhere else for a while, so I can try to get my head cleared? Or stay in here if you want; that's fine. But you have to be quiet."

Pammy jumped up. "I'll be back in a bit with some snacks. That'll give me time to think of what else Mitch said and give you a minute to yourself."

༄༅

This Diary Belongs to:

Rebekah Sue Lang

ENTRY DATE: Sunday, July 7, 1968

How is it even possible that we just got here yesterday?

I feel like at least a week has happened. Today was insane. If I wrote in here earlier today it would be all about saving Pammy from a creep, but we've moved from that to being saved from sin.

I am so completely confused about everything right now. But Pammy doesn't seem confused at all. It's like she's discovered some long-lost answer to a question I never knew she was asking. She seems different. Like not a care in the world. But Pammy didn't have any cares to begin with. Not like I do.

I think I just want to go home. I don't want to stay here for the whole month. I want to go home and read Johnny's letters and listen to my song over and over. I'm gonna talk to Mama and Daddy about it. I think they'll understand. Even if I don't completely understand myself.

Oh man!! I forgot about the cheerleading camp for Pammy. Darn it!! I guess we have to stay after all.

I am just too sad to write anymore now.

Rebekah closed the diary, locked it and placed it back in her suitcase, being sure to return the key to the secret pocket under the lining. It made her feel like she had something of value to hide from others, even if she knew that was far from the case.

She used to think her parents and even Pammy were dying to find out all her secrets, but she figured out a long time ago that it was almost impossible for her to keep her thoughts secret—since she wore her heart on her sleeve.

She read that somewhere about Scarlett O'Hara's character. Scarlett was outspoken and temperamental. Scarlett probably would have benefitted from keeping a diary. It does help to keep some secrets secret.

Like her biggest secret of all!

One day she was going to be Rebekah Sue Rizzo. She just wasn't sure when to tell Johnny.

☙❧

Monday, July 8, 1968

"All I Have to Do Is Dream"

Rebekah woke early but hardly refreshed. For the first time in longer than she could remember, one of those pesky dreams had invaded her sleep. As annoying as they were and as disturbed as they left her, she still retraced them in her mind in an effort to piece it all together. Dreams could rarely, if ever, be pieced together, but she could not stop herself from trying.

She sat up in bed and closed her eyes, remembering . . .

She and Pammy and many other folks, like teachers and cousins and random people she couldn't quite place, were bowling. The bowling lane was like some kind of obstacle course with three very narrow openings to select for the ball to go through to begin its journey down the lane. Pammy and the others on the team got all strikes. Rebekah was the last one to bowl, and everything depended on her to keep their team in the lead.

After taking the two steps and maneuvering the ball back in preparation to bring it forward and let it go, she looked up to see three people standing at the end of the alley. In her estimation, she was to aim the ball in such a way as to avoid hitting the people while still leveling all the pins for the strike. She was the only one who seemed to be aware this was an impossible assignment. Someone was bound to get hurt, and she would be the one doing the hurting. Instead of aiming for the pins—or the people—she deliberately threw gutter balls.

Several versions of the scenario played out before Pammy got so mad at her that she fumed, pacing back and forth and screaming she didn't appreciate Rebekah causing her to waste her three dollars with nothing to show for it.

The nonsensical dream ended with Rebekah telling Pammy she would give her the three dollars back.

It also left Rebekah fully aware that Pammy had decided that their friendship was over and fully aware that she meant over *forever*. Walking away, weighed down by hopelessness, she caught sight of everyone—now, including her mother—laughing.

And smoking pot together.

Rebekah shook off the dream but couldn't quite shake off the unsettled feeling permeating through her body and mind.

"Born to Be Wild"

As was usually the case, Rebekah's dream didn't line up with reality. But sometimes reality seemed more like a dream. Such as when her best friend, who was furious with her the day before and even refused to speak to her, suddenly acted as if the events of the previous day never even happened. Pammy had obviously been quite eager to talk at length about the previous night as soon as her eyes popped open.

Rebekah, on the other hand, could not so easily erase the memory of the day. Or of the dream. She heard very little of Pammy's monologue as they set up for another day on the beach.

As she slathered the Coppertone Oil over her chest, tummy and legs—making a mental note that it was noticeably time to shave again—Rebekah casually questioned her friend. "Have you ever smoked marijuana?"

"What?"

"Have you ever smoked marijuana?"

Pammy laughed. "Pretty sure you would know if I had."

"Well, not necessarily. I didn't know you smoked cigarettes, remember?"

"Mmm . . . that's true." Pammy had the decency to blush. "What do you think?"

"I think maybe you have. You know why I think so?"

"Good grief, Rebekah. What kinda game are you playing now?" Pammy rolled her eyes.

"No game. I was just thinking how you've been hanging around Kevin a lot, and we both know he's a bad influence." There, she finally brought up the Kevin subject again. She knew she had to. And even after he seemed super understanding when she practically sent him to the hospital, she still didn't trust him. She was about to find out if Pammy honestly felt the same way.

"I know what you're thinking of, but Kevin was just messin' with you in the pavilion the other night." Pammy surprised Rebekah with her response.

"He *told* you?"

"Yep. His friend dared him to act like a guy they had seen in some TV movie. They had been planning to use his stupid pick-up lines the first chance they got, but then Kevin almost backed out. So, Tim—that's his friend's name—dared him to and bet him lunch at the diner. He told me about it yesterday on our walk." Pammy bit her bottom lip.

"Who knew good old, quiet and boring Tim had it in him to set up a girl he didn't know like that? And then had the nerve to ask me to dance. I guess they were both jerks, huh?"

"Yeah, but at least Kevin is a repentant jerk," Pammy pointed out.

"Speaking of repentant, I thought of some more stuff that Mitch was telling us."

"I'm not so much wanting to talk about that right this minute. Just want to listen to music and clear my mind."

Rebekah reached into her bag for a cigarette.

"So, do you still smoke, or did you find out it's a sin?" Rebekah asked.

"Well, Mitch didn't talk about that. I don't think it's a sin per se. Pretty sure God would say it's not good for us, but I don't know if it's in the Bible."

The two of them sat quietly, elbows to knees, cigarettes to lips and thoughts to themselves until they puffed the last puff at the same time and lay back to the sound of Steppenwolf's "Born to Be Wild."

Instead of singing along, Rebekah lay in silence contemplating whether everyone was indeed born to be wild. Which made her contemplate whether she would ever smoke pot. Or if Johnny would.

Or why *anyone* would, actually.

"Sound of Silence"

"I'm getting baptized in a few hours," Pammy announced.

Rebekah thought she might be talking in her sleep even though Pammy's eyes were open, and she was sitting up again. She looked at her friend with raised eyebrows. Did she have a stroke or something? Had the sun been too much for her? Was she going to faint again? Maybe she just hadn't noticed that Pammy always said something bizarre right before fainting.

Rebekah read an article about a girl who had fainting spells and was diagnosed with something called syncope. Maybe that's what was wrong with Pammy. The article didn't mention anything about the girl saying weird things before she fainted, but maybe Pammy had double syncope or something. She would have to look it up to see if there was such a thing. If there wasn't, then maybe Pammy was the first.

"Pammy, are you feeling like you're going to faint?" Rebekah asked.

"No . . . , why?"

"I don't know, just wondering." Rebekah figured she could put that theory to rest—for now.

"Did you hear me? I'm getting baptized. So is Kevin and some others too," Pammy continued.

"Okay, so what does that mean? I kinda know, but not exactly. So go ahead and fill me in." Obviously, Pammy was determined to talk about it.

"The Bible says that we are to repent from our sins and turn to God. And be baptized in the name of Jesus. Mitch explained that baptism is an act of obedience to God's word and like making a statement that you're saved. So, we are going to be baptized in the ocean later. You should come too."

Rebekah raised her eyebrows. "Aren't you scared?"

"Why would I be scared?" Pammy asked.

"Because you're so afraid of the water. Or did you forget about that?"

"Oh, yeah, I guess I'm a little scared of that. But I'm more excited than I am scared."

Rebekah didn't know what else to say because the whole thing was just so all-of-a-sudden. Pammy was really serious about all of it, that much was for sure. She honestly had never heard Pammy talk about anything so much.

Rebekah considered going just to find out more about the baptism thing, but she kept it to herself. If she even mentioned it to Pammy, the whole thing would blow up like it was some big deal, which it absolutely was not.

They sat quietly lost in their own thoughts for a while. Long enough for each to smoke another cigarette. It didn't go unnoticed by Rebekah that Pammy's last puff was inhaled more deeply and held much longer than usual. Maybe she was having second thoughts about it being a sin after all and had told herself that was the last one—or not. Rebekah watched as Pammy pulled out another one and lit it up before the long-held puff had fully escaped.

"Wow. You didn't waste any time lighting up again, did you? Are we having a contest? 'Cause if so, it's not fair that you didn't let me know ahead of time," Rebekah lectured her friend.

"Huh? Oh, no contest. I've been sitting here thinking about getting into the water later, and I'm not feelin' so good. I feel like I'm gonna be sick or something. I need to calm myself down. I guess I really am scared. I need you to be there with me." Pammy looked a bit ashen to Rebekah.

"You don't have to do it, you know."

Since Pammy didn't respond, Rebekah almost continued with words of encouragement that would let Pammy know there was no law or rule being broken if she changed her mind.

But she remained silent—something Rebekah was not particularly known for—and she was as puzzled by this as much as anyone else would be.

☙ ❧

This Diary Belongs to:

Rebekah Sue Rizzo

ENTRY DATE: Wednesday, July 10, 1968

*It think it's fun to use the last name that will be mine soon—**HOPEFULLY!!!***

I couldn't even write about anything until now. And I'm still not sure exactly how to talk about the past few days. We'll take Pammy to cheerleading camp in less than a week, and I'm gonna ask Mama and Daddy if we can please just go home when we pick her up the next week.

That will be almost two more weeks here. I hope they go by really, really fast. But I don't know how that can happen with Pammy gone. I wonder what Donna's up to. I wish she could come down for that week. I know she can't, just wishful thinking!

Well, I went with Pammy 'cause she asked me to. I felt so stupid. Everybody there was getting baptized except me. Me and the band group and Rhonda. Rhonda was there, helping Mitch out in the water.

I didn't talk to her though. After Pammy got baptized and came up to talk to me about it, I just came on back here to the cottage. Pammy was nervous when it was her turn to go into the water and Rhonda took her arm and walked with her to about waist deep. Then Mitch talked to her about how baptism doesn't save anybody, only believing in Jesus Christ as your Savior does that. But baptism is an outward expression of your inward decision to believe and follow Jesus with all your heart. That's what Pammy told me he said anyway.

And then she told me that she does believe it and that as soon as she got out in the water, she had no fear or nervousness or anything. She said she felt completely calm and peaceful. I thought that was such a strange word for her to use. But peaceful does sound wonderful.

Before Pammy went out, I watched some others. I still can't say I completely understand all of it, but I will say that every single bit of it seemed real and not like a put-on show or fake.

I'm gonna ask Johnny if he ever got baptized.

"Heaven Must Have Sent You"

The week before taking Pammy to camp went by faster than Rebekah feared it would. She was pretty surprised herself that she was counting the days until she would be back home. When exactly did the beach stop being her Shangri-la? Maybe the beach itself never really was. Maybe she built it up to be something it wasn't. The first time she heard about Shangri-la, was when she tried to read *Lost Horizon*, but it was just too much for her. She was a little disappointed in herself for not finishing it—not getting very far into it at all.

She did look up the definition to learn that Shangri-la was an imaginary place. At some point she must have convinced herself that it wasn't imaginary at all but was very real and had been right there all along—Myrtle Beach.

But that was yesterday, so to speak, and like Chad and Jeremy said, "Yesterday's Gone." This thought track was bringing her way down. She metaphorically "slapped herself across the cheek" to bring her out of the morose disposition—*morose* was a great word but not at all a really great feeling.

The week did bring some changes. Pammy told her that after she was baptized, she decided not to smoke anymore. She said it wasn't because she thought it was a sin, but she just didn't want to do something she thought God might not want her to. She assured Rebekah that she didn't expect her to do the same.

Rebekah wasn't considering doing the same, even if her friend did expect her to. But it was good to know Pammy wasn't going to hold it against her. They sat on the beach watching boys and girls walking hand-in-hand and little ones filling and emptying bright plastic buckets of sand while mothers, with one eye trained on them, tried to relax. Finally, Rebekah lit her first cigarette and broached the subject.

"Isn't it hard to quit?" she asked Pammy.

"Smoking? Not really. But I did smoke a few before I decided to stop. I'm not so sure if I decided to quit or if somehow God kinda "told" me to. It's hard to explain, but I feel like He really knows me and wants the best for me. I don't know. It's hard to explain." Pammy's answer was longer than Rebekah expected.

"I'm not totally against it—against God. But I just need time to think about it all. And I'm gonna talk to Johnny about it too."

"I get that. But don't take too long, Rebekah. Because I believe it's absolutely true what Mitch said. And he said it's in the Bible too," Pammy warned.

"What's absolutely true?"

"That none of us knows how long we have to live. People die at all ages, from babies to really old folks. And if we're old enough to know about Jesus but die without believing in Him as our Savior, we won't go to Heaven. There is a Heaven, and there is a Hell, and we are all going to one or the other."

"Wow. That's harsh. Why would God send us to Hell?"

"I don't think He does that. I think we just have a lot to learn. I'm gonna go to the church that Mitch told us about. You wanna come with me?" asked Pammy.

"Maybe." That was all Rebekah was willing to commit to.

This Diary Belongs to:

Rebekah Sue Rizzo

ENTRY DATE: Monday, July 15, 1968

*I've been writing my new (SOON) name on stuff so much, I have to remind myself it's not my name **yet**!*

So, we dropped Pammy off at camp this morning. Please, please let time fly by!!

Mama said that since Pammy is gone for the week, we should hang out together and do some stuff. Hmm??? I wonder what kinda stuff she wants to do. I can't think of anything that she does that I'd want to do too, by myself or with her! Please, please don't be cards.

Something crazy happened yesterday. Pammy and I went to the church that Mitch told her about. And there he was and the others from the band, up on the stage playing music. No Beatles or Elvis songs. They were churchy songs. I didn't know any of them. But they weren't too bad.

The preacher (I think that's what he's called) talked about how different people from the Bible did some pretty bad things, but God still loved them. Then he talked about how God didn't just love them, but that He used them to tell others about Himself. He basically said that God loves us no matter what we've done, and He wants us to be with Him now and in Heaven after we leave this earth.

At the end, they passed a bowl around for anybody who wanted to give money to the "ministry" (that's what he called it), but he said if it was your first time there to not give because you are their guest. That was me and Pammy. But I gave a dollar anyway. Not sure why I did though.

Then he talked some about Jesus and how knowing Him is how we get into Heaven. He said a prayer and asked anyone who wanted to repent of their sin and believe that Jesus died for them to raise their hand. Everybody's eyes were closed, and I did it!!!

I raised my hand because I do want to go to heaven. But then when everybody opened their eyes, he asked everyone who raised their hand to come to the front where he was standing.

I didn't do that. I was nervous and scared. But now I think I might have missed my chance and it's too late to do anything about it. I'm gonna ask Johnny about it. I'm so scared that if I did miss my chance, then Johnny might not want to be with me.

Oh, please, please don't let that be true!!!

"Mama Said"

A light tap on the bedroom door shifted Rebekah's attention away from her diary. She slapped it closed and tucked it under the mattress with a mental note to retrieve it as soon as possible. But at the thought of forgetting it, she got it back out and tucked it behind her pillow.

"Come in," she said.

"Hi, sweetie, just checking on you. I brought you some lunch. Are

Part 3: Summer 1968

you feeling sad and lonely without Pammy here? Seems strange, huh?" Her mother seemed nervous. She was rattling on and on.

"I'm okay. I wanted to ask you and Daddy something, though, speaking of Pammy being gone and picking her up in a week." Rebekah realized that her mother hadn't said anything about picking Pammy up, but she wanted to get to the point. Get it settled. If she knew they would be going home in one week, she would be willing to do pretty much anything her mother wanted. Even play cards, if necessary.

Maybe she should use that as leverage . . . "Sure, I'll do (fill in the blank) with you, Mama, as long as we go home next Sunday."

As her mother handed her the lunch plate—featuring a still-warm tuna melt, Rebekah told her it could have been featured in a food magazine. On the cover, for that matter. The cheddar cheese was slightly toasted, bubbly and running off the edge onto the plate where Rebekah would be scooping it up with the barbeque potato chips that always accompanied her second favorite sandwich of all time. Well, perhaps tied with the grilled cheese now that she had discovered her own signature sandwich. But if she was being honest with herself, she would have to admit that her own creation was a distant third.

"What did you want to ask about, dear?"

"Where is Daddy, anyway?" Rebekah preferred to ask both of them at the same time. That way one or the other was more likely to empathize with her than taking a chance with a one-on-one conversation.

"He's gone to do some fishing." Her mother paused briefly before adding, "So it's the perfect time for you and me to do something. What would you like to do? You name it, and we'll do it," she promised.

"Great." Rebekah covered her tuna-filled, opened mouth. "Let's go get my Mustang. It can be an early graduation present. I can't believe it. You said anything, right? Thank you, thank you, thank you."

"Rebekah Louise! You know I didn't mean that literally."

"I do now . . . since you used my full name."

"Seriously, is there anything special you can think of? Anything you've wanted to do but haven't yet?"

Rebekah thought about it for a few minutes while she finished her lunch. She didn't know if she could come up with anything she would really want to do that her mother would be willing—or able—to do with her.

And then it hit her.

"Yes, there is something that I've been wanting to do for a really long time. And it's not something I ever thought we would do together—but we should."

"Oh, dear, I hope I haven't gotten myself into something I will live to regret," her mother replied teasingly.

"Oh How Happy"

Sitting directly across from each other, they had been rocking back and forth with the rhythm of the gentle waves for a while when Rebekah noticed her mother tearing up. Oh, brother, this was supposed to be fun.

They had purchased the two-seater rubber boat/float at K-Mart just before leaving town. Rebekah had thought about trying to talk Pammy into getting out in the surf with it, but there never seemed to be a good time to bring it up.

The perfect solution was already starting to feel like the air was quickly leaking out of it—that is, the air that took both her and her mother about twenty minutes to pump into it. Even using a bicycle tire pump was awkward and slow. Neither one of them had ever used a pump before. The couple of times that Rebekah had tried before, her father got impatient and insisted on doing it for her.

He was a really great daddy in so many ways, but he was not good at all about teaching her the how-tos of life. Maybe if she was a boy he would have wanted to. She guessed her mother's dad must have been the same. Didn't they say that girls usually marry fellas that are like their daddies? She didn't want to think about whether Johnny was like her own father. That was just too weird. And gross.

She didn't want to know, but she knew she had to ask, "Mama, why are you crying?"

"Oh, dear," she replied, "I'm sorry sweetheart, it's just that I'm really happy. Just you and me. Mother and daughter. This, here with you is the happiest I've been in a really long time."

"Seriously?" Rebekah completely understood why something as silly as bouncing up and down on a really cool boat float would make her happy, but she never imagined that being the thing that would make her mother happier than she had been in a really long time. Man, she must have been pretty miserable. She kinda wanted to know why but not really. She said a little prayer to please help them to just have a nice time and not get into any heavy-duty conversations. Everything had been going great for a good while now.

Let's not spoil our record and get all emotional. Especially out here. There's nowhere to run. No escape. Please don't let her have some kind of emotional breakdown. Not here. Not now.

"Come on, let's paddle a little farther out so the waves won't have us crashing into the shore," Rebekah suggested to change their focus.

"Okay, what do I do?" her mother asked, dabbing the corners of her eyes.

Rebekah explained exactly how they should each paddle with

their open palms to turn in the direction necessary to maneuver farther out. Whether she simply did not explain it clearly or whether her mother simply did not understand—or both—whatever the reason, they found themselves working as hard as they could to do nothing but go around and around in very slow circles. The small waves added an element reminiscent of a carnival ride. Up and down. Around and around.

If it hadn't felt so out-of-control and unpredictable, they might have abandoned any attempts to stick with the original plan and gleefully embraced the thrill. But they kept at it, furiously paddling with only their hands.

The harder they tried, the more they spun. And the more they spun, the heartier they laughed. They laughed so hard they had no clue exactly where they were until they were both violently flipped out onto shore where they lay until they were able to stop laughing.

"Well, that didn't go as planned, did it? Wanna try again?" Rebekah asked her mother, who had pulled herself up and made her way out of the shallow water to the edge of the shoreline.

"I . . . think I better . . . call it quits . . . for now. I'm afraid I may have . . . done something . . . to my arm." She winced with each word.

"Oh, no." Rebekah took one look at her arm and knew something wasn't right. "I'll go find Daddy. You wait right here." She jumped up and ran off in the direction of the pier, but her mother called her back.

"Let's just get back to the cottage, and I'll put some ice on it. I'm sure it's nothing serious."

Rebekah debated whether to obey. She hadn't once seen her mother in any kind of pain. Not even the time when her mother was leaning over her while Rebekah was experiencing a seizure brought on by a high fever, and Rebekah chomped down on her mother's arm, drawing blood. She would hear about it later and see the horrible mark it left, but even though she caused it, she didn't technically witness her mother's pain.

Her mother never even had a headache before, at least not that Rebekah was aware of. She hadn't really thought about it before, but seeing her like that, in such obvious discomfort, made Rebekah very uneasy.

Until that very moment, she had no idea her mother's excellent health and injury-free life had been a huge part of her own stability. It had given her a sense of security she'd been unaware of until that moment.

"Rebekah, I'm fine, dear. See, I can hold my arm up against me." Her mother showed her as she used her good arm like a sling. "You grab the float, and we'll be back at the cottage in no time. I'm okay. Okay?"

Fine. She'd do what her mother said.

"If I Fell"

Thankfully, Rebekah's father was back from fishing. He wasted no time in grabbing a bath towel to use as a makeshift splint.

"How did you do this?"

Her mother winced. "Rebekah and I were having so much fun in the new boat. But the waves tossed us right out of it, and I landed on my arm. Do you think it's broken?"

Rebekah hadn't considered her mother's injury might be *that* serious. But her father wasn't willing to guess. He insisted he take her to the hospital just to be sure. Rebekah had never seen a broken arm, but she certainly knew enough about it to know it was a minor injury in the scheme of things.

But her father's nervousness and worrisome expression made her wonder if she had missed something. Maybe a broken arm could lead to other things—but that made no sense. So, maybe a broken arm was a sign of some underlying condition or disease—that made no sense either. Or did it? She watched as her father lovingly and tenderly assisted her mother into the car. She watched the car until it was out of sight. Her mother looked so frail.

Rebekah would not allow her ridiculous imagination to take over. She was hungry. And lonely. She would grab some comfort food. She couldn't remember where she had heard or seen that term before, but it was certainly fitting for the moment.

First, she carefully arranged the comfort foods—Sue's Peanut Butter Sandwich Surprise, a handful of potato chips, and a glass of milk—on the bed, then placed the stack of Johnny's letters beside her. With Ralphie snuggled next to her, Rebekah sank into the pillow behind her and let out a deep, audible breath. She was ready to concentrate on something other than her mother's plight. She would know the details soon enough, but for now she would turn her attention to the longing in her heart. But first, several bites to tend to her gnawing stomach.

She was now ready to read Johnny's letters one by one. Starting with the one that came the day before leaving home. Somehow, she had managed not to open it yet. She wasn't at all confident she could do it, but she wanted to wait to read them when it would be just her and him together—in her mind a least—no one else around, no one interrupting.

And there she was. She had managed to pull it off. She held the envelope against her face hoping for a hint of Johnny's scent. Did she really smell his aftershave, or was it her imagination? Either way, a surge of euphoria filled her.

She ran her index finger under the flap and pulled out the one-page letter. She was torn between the eager anticipation of reading it and the sheer delight of actually doing so. She wanted to hold onto both emotions as long as she could.

These feelings were like the ones she experienced as a child when such feelings confused her. If she got a new set of colored pencils, she couldn't wait to try them all out, but at the same time she wanted to keep them new and perfect. She had relayed this, as best she could, to her father, who'd told her, "Rebekah, my girl, you are learning one of life's toughest lessons. You can't have your cake and eat it too."

What having and eating cake had to do with using or keeping her pencils new made about as much sense to her as, "Don't count your chickens before they hatch." Even still, years later, she didn't have a clear understanding of either.

She unfolded the paper and read each word at a slow, deliberate pace.

June 15, 1968

My Sweet Rebekah Sue,

I think about you all the time. I guess by the time you read this, you'll be getting ready to go to the beach. I think about us together at the beach all the time too. The only thing I could say that's similar, and it's a really big stretch, is that it's hot here too. It rains a lot, but it's not like it cools anything down. Just turns this sauna into a steam bath.

Being here is so strange. In lots of ways, but especially lately. We have days and days of sitting around waiting and then all of a sudden, we're going full speed ahead to accomplish something that urgently needed to be done—like yesterday—even though we could have been working on it all along if somebody had just told us. It's pretty frustrating.

Word is floating around about some BIG operation soon. Pretty sure that means I will at least be up in the chopper doing what I've been trained to do. Yeah, it's dangerous, but I'm not worried about that. We know what we're doing, and when we have a job to do, you better believe it's gonna be done right.

I don't know why I'm even saying all that to you. I've gone back and forth on what I really want to say, Rebekah. I'm just gonna put myself out there and say it because it's all I think about, and I need to know (one way or the other) what you think.

So here goes . . . It really stinks to do this in a letter, and I promise you when I get home, I will do this proper, but for now I gotta know.

Rebekah Sue, will you marry me?

I Sure Do Love You,
Johnny

ঌ৯

Sunday, July 21, 1968

"Homeward Bound"

They were back home in Raleigh before Rebekah opened either of the other two letters from Johnny. She came home to three more.

Once it was determined that Rebekah's mother had indeed broken her arm, her father insisted that they go home as soon as they picked Pammy up from camp. The relief of this change of plans and the incredible letter from Johnny had her "walking on cloud nine," another expression that she had not completely understood before this. She absolutely understood it now.

She kept the details of his letter to herself. Hidden in her heart. She would share with the world soon enough, and with her best friend even sooner, but for the time being, she just wanted to bask in what she and Johnny alone were aware of: Wedding bells were in their future.

Before receiving his proposal letter, she had written and torn up more letters than she could count. Letters containing the words that could best tell Johnny how much she loved him. Ones filled with promises to wait for him forever. And the hardest of all to articulate was how she dreamed of being Mrs. Johnny Rizzo one day—a day that she hoped and dreamed would be as soon after he got back as possible.

Her Johnny Bean had relieved her of that impossible mission. Thankfully, he couldn't hold back any longer than she could.

Rebekah had already written her "yes" letter and mailed it to him from the beach. She really wanted to see Rhonda again; she would have told Rhonda about Johnny's proposal and her acceptance. She would have told Rhonda that she'd be invited to their wedding. But Rhonda was not at the shop at all the rest of that week.

In the privacy of her own bedroom, a stack of 45s ready to go with the turn of the dial, Rebekah sat, legs crisscrossed in front of her, with the five remaining letters stacked in order of postmark date. She was ready to read any other news Johnny had to share.

Everything she read from then on would be in light of the future Mr. and Mrs. Johnny Rizzo.

"Mr. and Mrs. Johnny Rizzo. Mrs. Rebekah Rizzo," she whispered, eyes closed. She had said it so many times, but this was the first time saying it out loud since knowing without a doubt that it was real.

One by one, starting with his letter dated June 17 and ending with the June 30 one, she read each word. Every "and," every "but," and every "if" were read with the same scrutiny as the words "battles," and "enemy fire," and "best buddy died today." By the time she finished reading the first two letters, it was all she could do to keep reading the remaining three.

❧❦

This Diary Belongs to:

Rebekah Sue Rizzo

ENTRY DATE: Monday, September 2, 1968

I can't believe that tomorrow is the first day of my senior year of high school. I am SO ready to be done. And to think that I will (hopefully) be getting married to my Johnny Bean soon after graduation is almost too hard to believe.

I keep wishing time away. Mostly because I just want Johnny to come home. Where he will be safe. He mentioned something about things "escalating" in his last couple of letters. He tries to be vague and he asks for prayer, but I can't help but have a bad feeling about everything he isn't saying. I SO hope I'm wrong.

Mama, Daddy, and I were supposed to have spent Labor Day weekend with Allen and his family. We had planned to go into DC for some sightseeing. That would have been fun. But Mama isn't feeling well; she said she has a bad cold. So Daddy will just grill some burgers and stuff. Pammy is coming over in about an hour.

I'm excited for us to talk about tomorrow and what to wear and all. It's all I can do to not tell her about the surprise that Mama and I have for her. But it hasn't arrived yet, so mum's the word!!

Part 3: Summer 1968

Friday, September 20, 1968

Oh, Johnny,

    I so wish you were here right now. No one else can console me.

    The most horrible thing has happened. I will never forget Wednesday, September 11th, even though I would give anything to be able to.

    Pammy is gone! My hands are shaking as I write those words. I feel like I am having an out-of-body experience. I've felt like that before—BUT NOTHING LIKE THIS!!

    We were at lunch messing around like we were acting out parts in a movie. And Pammy stood up and mumbled something and then fell straight back onto the floor. We thought she was just being overly dramatic. We all laughed!

    One of the cafeteria ladies rushed over and did CPR on her. Johnny, it just can't be real, can it? Please tell me it isn't. Please tell me I just had the worst nightmare I could ever have. That none of this is really happening!!

    I cry every day, and I can't go back to school. How could I? How can I keep living without her?

    They said her heart just gave out. Like she probably had a defect or something, maybe since she was born. But nobody knew. How can that be possible? How could I not have known?

    We didn't even get to give her the outfits. Mama and I had thumbed through the Sears Catalog for hours, picking out the perfect outfits to give to her. Kind of a congratulations on making cheerleading. We didn't want her to think of it as charity or something. I just really, really wanted to do something good. And it felt really good. Way better than picking out stuff for myself!!

    We were expecting the package to arrive any day before school started, but it only arrived in time for her funeral. Her mama decided to dress her in the black and red and cream plaid kilt skirt with the cream turtleneck and black button-down cardigan sweater. She also picked the matching cream tights and cute black loafers. She said she wanted her to be warm. Some people said she looked like she was just sleeping. I didn't look at her. I couldn't.

I don't know what Mama did with the rest of the clothes. I don't want to know. I don't care—they were supposed to be Pammy's!!

My heart is broken beyond repair.

I hope you can write back to me right away. It was so hard reading the last letters that I got from you. It sounds like you are doing really dangerous stuff. I know you are! And when I don't hear from you for so long, well—I can't even write about that!

Just please write back SOON!

I love you and I can't wait to be your wife!

Yours forever and always,
Rebekah

January 15, 1969

"The Letter"

Rebekah had disliked the month of January as long as she could remember. All the excitement of Christmas seemed to dissolve into nothingness as soon as the gifts were opened. This year added another level of lackluster to the typically dull winter; it had been weeks since her last letter from Johnny. She had written very little in her diary because she was writing letters to Johnny every single day. She must have mailed ten or more since she heard from him last.

She dropped Donna off at a friend's house after school. They were going to study together and though they had invited Rebekah to join them, she declined. The dark, snowy-looking day had her just wanting to get home. And check the mail. And prepare her heart to face the empty mailbox—again.

She parked the car and got out, in no particular hurry. She considered walking right past the mailbox to avoid the disappointment. But her high hopes always trumped those feelings when it came to any chance of anything involving her guy.

Her hands shook as she removed the large envelope. She stared for several seconds at his handwriting. She had missed it. She ran straight to her room and threw herself across the bed and tore open the envelope, removing the letter with such haste she almost tore it in half. She rolled onto her back and held it to her chest before rolling back over to read the words she'd been longing for.

December 2, 1968

To the future Mrs. Johnny Rizzo,

Hello, my love. I hope you get this by Christmas. I'm watching out for the one you said you would be sending right after Thanksgiving. Nothing yet, but I'm sure it's on its way.

I hope you like your gift. I couldn't believe that I was able to get my hands on something so beautiful in this God-forsaken place.

Things are pretty quiet right now. But we never know how long that will last.

No matter what, do not ever forget that I love you! I love you more every single day.

I need another picture soon. The one I have has been everywhere I've been, and it shows. It's dirty and torn and in need of some R & R. Ha! Ha! So send me that replacement soon.

Now, imagine hearing me scream this 'cause I am . . .
"I LOVE REBEKAH SUE LANG!" *and* "I LOVE THE FUTURE REBEKAH SUE RIZZO!!!"
I'll write again as soon as I can,

All my love — all the time,
Johnny

❧ ☙

Rebekah's gentle smile became a beaming grin as she opened the box. A small handwritten note attached to the top read, "The minute I see you, we will replace this with a genuine engagement ring. In the meantime, I sure hope you like this, and I sure hope it fits."

Her beaming grin turned to tears of joy as she lifted the lid to reveal the gift. She closed her eyes, and pictured Johnny on one knee. "Yes!" She answered his imaginary question out loud as she slipped the beautiful pearl ring on her left finger.

After staring at it for some time, she jumped up and ran to the kitchen to show her mother. Not finding her, she peeked through the window overlooking the garden where her mother could usually be found when not in the kitchen. She wasn't there either. Then she heard her parents' voices coming from their bedroom.

Just before she excitedly knocked on the door, she heard what sounded like her mother crying. Maybe she would come back later. Maybe they were having an argument, although she hadn't heard anything close to that for years.

They weren't speaking loudly, but as she turned to tiptoe back to her bedroom, she clearly heard just one word from her mother's crackling voice . . . cancer.

Part 4:
Spring 1969

Tuesday, March 11, 1969

"Be True to Your School"

It had been six months since she lost Pammy.

Rebekah sat with elbows propped on her desk and chin resting in her cupped hands. She had been staring at the world history book, trying to read about the Battle of Stalingrad, considered to be the most brutal battle of World War II. But battles and wars were the last thing she wanted to read or think about. She closed the book, brought her hands together and prayed. If there was a proper way to do so, she did not know what it was, but she hoped her prayers for Johnny's safety were acceptable to God.

Somehow, she had managed to go back to school. Since it was the senior year, she needed only three class credits to graduate. They were easy classes for her. It was a good thing too, because it was all she could do to show up every day and try to pay attention in class.

Lucky for them, Donna had the same schedule. As soon as the end-of-third bell rang, they would meet up behind the gym at the back of the school and smoke a cigarette in honor and memory of Pammy. Even though Pammy had decided to quit smoking, they did it for her anyway because they were pretty sure she had still wanted to smoke; she just hadn't wanted to disappoint God.

Rebekah's parents had gotten her a car just before school started, Never mind that it wasn't the Mustang she had dreamed of for so long. She was perfectly content with her brand-new Volkswagen Beetle. It wasn't powder blue, but she loved the bright Poppy Red. It was cheerful, and if anyone wanted and needed cheering up it was Rebekah Louise (Sue) Lang.

Before that terrible day, she had picked Pammy up each morning for school. She often wondered—whenever she thought back to the few car rides they had before "it" happened—if Pammy somehow had an idea that something had been wrong. She talked a lot about how happy she was to be a cheerleader even though she might not be able to do it for very long. Rebekah assumed she was referring to the fact that she only had their last year of school to enjoy it. She told Rebekah she was glad she quit smoking because she didn't want to get kicked off the squad, but now Rebekah wondered if she quit because she was having trouble breathing or something. Of course, she would never know. But it gave some comfort to remember that Pammy also talked about Heaven and knowing Jesus.

Rebekah started picking Donna up and planned to do so for the remainder of the school year. Sometimes, they would smoke in her new car too. Rebekah didn't worry about her parents knowing because they didn't know how to drive a car with a clutch. She found it a bit ironic that she'd taught herself how to drive it since her daddy couldn't. Maybe she'd teach him some day—if she figured out how to get rid of the stale smoke odor.

The humdrum school year continued. Rebekah just plugged along, counting the days until graduation on June 2. As she marked off the school days on the wall calendar that hung on her bedroom closet door, she also marked the dates—with a heart—when she received letters from Johnny.

❧ ❦

This Diary Belongs to:

Rebekah Sue Rizzo

(SOON I hope)

Saturday, March 22, 1969

I've received five letters from Johnny since school started. The last one is from February 3. He hasn't written many details; but in his last one, he mentioned something about his helicopter being under fierce fire when they were attempting to rescue some soldiers trapped behind enemy lines. That's what he called it. Fierce Fire!!! He didn't mention if they'd been successful. That makes me think they probably weren't.

It's getting so hard to concentrate at school because I'm worried about him. I hope, hope, hope I get a letter soon!!

He was devastated by the news of Pammy's passing. He told me he was at a loss for words, but his heart hurt for "his girl."

All our letters since his proposal have included wedding plans. He teased me about the honeymoon he was saving up for. He said "it's gonna take a big ole fat wad of cash," and he couldn't wait to surprise me. And my only hint . . . pack plenty of swimsuits.

I've already been looking at the Sears Catalog and found a few.
I can barely think about anything else at all!!

❧❦

May 1969

"Everything's Alright"

Rebekah hadn't said one word to anyone, including Donna, about what she and her parents had been dealing with. The only person she would have confided in was Pammy. And Johnny. She did write to him about it, but she hadn't heard back from him.

She was excited to hear what he thought of the picture she sent him. She was sitting on the blue rayon armchair in their living room, her long, straight blonde hair parted down the middle and flowing past her shoulders, with her left hand held in front of her—the perfectly fitted pearl ring shining. Her glowing smile reflected all the love, anticipation, and joy their life together would bring.

She jumped from her car, checked the empty mailbox and headed right in to check on her mother.

A few weeks ago, her parents had told her about her mother's illness. She had been diagnosed with breast cancer about four months before the afternoon when Rebekah heard her crying. Her mother confessed she had known something was wrong long before the day it was diagnosed, but she had kept it to herself as long as she could. Rebekah had noticed that ever since the broken arm, her father barely let her mother out of his sight.

He told Rebekah he had sensed that her mother was not well but wanted to wait for her to talk to him. He then told her that his decision was changed after the doctor visit for her broken arm. On the day of the ER visit, the doctor wanted to do some bloodwork and run a few tests in addition to treating the broken arm. Rebekah's mother adamantly had insisted that extra tests were completely unnecessary.

He also explained to Rebekah that her mother's strong opposition caused much concern for him. He felt just as strongly that if the doctor thought it was a good idea, then she absolutely should do it.

Since the horrible day when Pammy died, Rebekah no longer took anything for granted. Her concern for her mother had her coming straight home from school. She was beside her mother every day while she fought her war on cancer. And Rebekah had no doubt that her mother would win, one battle at a time. Surely she would not lose her best friend and her mother within months of each other. She truly believed that everything would be alright.

She spent her alone time, just before bed, listening to one song over and over. The words defined her. Oh how she longed to hold the hand of her loving man. She needed him to come home. She clung to the belief that "Everything's Alright."

But it wasn't.

Eloise Geraldine Adams Lang died at 5:55 p.m. on Wednesday, May 21, 1969, at fifty years of age with her devoted husband and loving daughter at her side.

※ ※

This Diary Belongs to:

Rebekah Sue

Tuesday, June 17, 1969

This is probably the last time I will write in here, or in any diary. I'm not sure why I'm even writing in it now. But here I am.

I wrote Rebekah Sue at the top because that is who I will always be. In my heart I'll always be Rebekah Sue Rizzo. But only in my heart.

I'll be eighteen on Saturday, June 21st, and I'll be married on Saturday, August 23, 1969.

I have to. He's all I have left. I've lost everyone. Even though my daddy is still alive, I lost him the day Mama died.

The day of Mama's funeral, I didn't know I'd be getting married in just a few months. Things can happen very quickly, and sometimes it's just for the best. Well, I take that back—it's not for the best, but it is my best option.

I tried to think about going to college to be a teacher, but I just can't. I just can't think about it all. When Mark told me that he loves me and that he's always loved me, I was pretty surprised. He told me he knows I don't love him the same way, but he wants to take care of me. His father owns some of the biggest car dealerships around, and Mark will go straight from high school into the business. He said he'll always be able to provide for me. Most folks would say that I'm a pretty lucky girl. But I did ask him if he loved me so much, why did he get with Donna. He said he didn't even know her before that day at the pool. She just came up and lay down next to him and started talking to him. Then when I pretty much dumped him, he decided he'd go out with her. But he never stopped liking me—loving me.

That's just so crazy to think about now. I wouldn't have even talked to Mark about anything if Johnny was still here. But Johnny isn't here, and he never will be again. I know he died. Otherwise, he would have written to me, but I never heard from him after February. My heart has no hope.

I know in my heart he is gone. I have no way to talk to his family, but I really don't need to. I'm numb. My heart is dead. I'll marry Mark and stop thinking about Johnny. But I will never stop wearing my pearl ring. That was stupid. Of course I'll never stop thinking about Johnny.

But Mark is sweet, and he's all I've got. I will marry Mark. I know he loves me. I don't know why, but I know he does. I will not be a burden to my poor daddy. He seems so lost. Of course he is, so am I. But we don't need to be lost together, as a constant reminder of what was and will never be again.

My brother offered to have me live with them, but I don't know; that doesn't seem best. I don't want to disrupt their family. I never did learn sign language either.

I'll end this by saying something I will never say to Mark, of course. I may never say it to anyone ever again, but I will say it here, probably in the last place and for the last time . . .

I have loved—I do love—and I will ALWAYS love Johnny Rizzo! And I will always—in my heart— be Mrs. Rebekah Sue Rizzo. ALWAYS!!! I hope that someday I can find out what happened to him.

☙❧

November 22, 2023

Office of Dr. Bradley J. Holcomb

Rebekah was just late enough to trouble Dr. Holcomb.

He had written many notes when he got home the night after their previous session. And had done some research into documented cases of prolonged stifled grief. Everything he read lined up with what he was witnessing in Rebekah's demeanor. But he sensed there was more. Such as, why she claimed responsibility for her friend's death.

He would begin that day's session—if indeed there still was to be a session—with that very question. The knock at the door assured him that there would be at least one more session.

"Come in. Hello, Rebekah, how are you doing today?" He stood as she entered and made her way to her new favorite seat.

"Hello, Dr. Holcomb. I'm sorry I'm late. I misjudged my time. I was baking pies for tomorrow, and I couldn't leave them. I should have called. Thanksgiving seems to sneak up on me every year."

"I'm just glad you are here. If you don't mind, I'd like to jump right in with a few questions." He wouldn't waste time with small talk.

Rebekah held onto her purse, stopping herself from picking at her cuticles. She briefly reflected on her "I stopped doing that and started doing this" list. She reminded herself that she started up again with the disgusting cuticle-picking after she quit smoking. Some people might replace smoking with drinking alcohol, but not Rebekah. Two sips of beer and one sip of wine over the years convinced her she had no interest in continuing to develop a taste for it. How silly.

It's perfectly fine if you just didn't enjoy something. She had, however, done just that—continued to develop a taste for it—when she decided to smoke from her mother's stash. But that was different. She was young and impressionable and much more ready and willing to push envelopes. One day she woke up to realize that pushing envelopes was a fool's game. That, and she suddenly, albeit a bit sadly, came to the realization that nobody really cared what she did nearly as much as she tended to think they did.

So, she'd decided to evaluate who exactly it is that she did "such and such" for. Even after concluding that she smoked cigarettes, first and foremost, because she really enjoyed smoking, all it took was one bad dream to change her mind.

One good check in the mirror proved that all her teeth were healthy and intact. The dream was like a visit from the ghost of Christmas future where she awakened with all her teeth missing. One by one, they rotted, crumbled, and fell out, with no hope of ever having anything but a gummy smile for the rest of her life. The birth of her precious granddaughter gave rebirth to the smile that she hadn't realized until then had been absent for quite some time.

"Rebekah, are you okay?" the doctor asked, with slightly raised voice.

"Oh, my. I'm so sorry, my mind was adrift. Please forgive me," she responded.

"Did you hear my question?" The slight shake of her head was his answer; thus he repeated it, "Can you tell me why you believe that you killed Pammy? That is your friend's name right, Pammy?"

Little time passed before she boldly answered, "I saw her. I heard her. I knew her. I was the one who convinced her to say nothing to anyone about almost drowning! I brushed it off when she fainted. More than once. I held our friendship over her head for one reason only—for one person only, I should say. Me! I wanted what I wanted. And I needed her to play my games to make it happen. If I had said something, or encouraged her to, she would have gotten help. The doctors could have discovered something wrong and fixed it."

Rebekah pursed her lips in hopes of holding back tears as she looked into the doctor's eyes once again and waited for him to chastise her, as she justly deserved. Surely, he would agree that her friend would likely be alive today if not for her selfish behavior.

The doctor sat studying her for several minutes.

"Rebekah, let me ask you this . . ." he began. He paused, retaining eye contact, and then continued: "If this scenario did not involve you and if your friend, Pammy, had done the things you say you did and someone else died from the identical cause, would you have blamed her for that person's death?"

Rebekah had no immediate answer. Based on her own rationale, she would have to. At the same time, she knew that would be terribly unfair. She needed more time to contemplate his question.

"My parents and I said a prayer together not long after Pammy died. I came into the living room while they were watching a Billy Graham special on TV. I had never heard of him. I had never heard anything like what he was saying. I'm sure they hadn't either."

Rebekah rose and returned to the window. A different car was parked where her daughter had parked earlier. With her car still in the shop, her daughter had insisted on driving her to her appointment with Dr. Holcomb. Rebekah imagined the baby had gotten fussy and that her daughter was driving around to soothe her. She had done that many times for her own child. Babies typically either loved riding in the car or they hated it. Lauren was quite thankful that her little Addie fit into the former category. Addie reminded Rebekah of Lauren when she was little in so many ways, but not in that way. Lauren hated riding in the car. Road trips were miserable for Lauren and for her.

Not so much for Rebekah's husband. He somehow managed to

tune everything out. This was a complete mystery to Rebekah because it wasn't as if he were in such a profound state of contemplation that he heard only his own thoughts. Far from it. He told her numerous times that he didn't have to be thinking about something all the time. And he added that when driving the car, he just concentrated on the road. Thus, he was able to ignore any crying.

She never said it but always thought that he was quite deft at ignoring music and conversation as well.

"I'm so sorry, my mind tends to wander. Anyway, at the end of the broadcast, Rev. Graham invited all who were watching to join in a prayer to turn to God and find a new life through his Son, Jesus Christ. Individually, the three of us spoke the prayer out loud with him, not knowing that each other would. We started going to church together the very next Sunday. The three of us were baptized shortly thereafter. Our lives changed completely in that sense."

Rebekah returned to her seat and sipped from the water bottle before continuing.

"I truly believed that since I had given my heart and my life to God, nothing bad would ever happen to me again. I wonder how many new believers believe such things. I now know that a relationship with God is built on trust in Him no matter what does or does not happen in our lives. But I did not understand that then. I felt that I had surely suffered enough with the loss of my Pammy. I believed that surely God would bring Johnny home soon. I believed the rest of my life would be blissful."

ನಿ ಈ

January 9, 2024

Office of Dr. Bradley J. Holcomb

"Have you thought any more about my question concerning the death of your friend? More specifically, about why you feel responsible?" Dr. Holcomb asked Rebekah after they exchanged pleasantries.

"I have. I've thought about what you said. I have some idea of why I've carried that belief for so many years," Rebekah replied.

"Good. Let's talk about that," he responded.

"I've heard folks talk about it, and I've read about folks who have had what they call a "crisis of faith," but I never quite understood what that would look like on a personal level. You see, I never stopped believing in God. I knew without a doubt, in my innermost being, that God was real. From the time I prayed the prayer with my parents in front of our TV that day, I never once stopped believing in Him."

Dr. Holcomb remained silent as Rebekah paused in thought.

"Do you know why I am so sure that I never stopped believing in Him?"

"Why?" the doctor asked.

"Because I was furious with Him. My anger toward Him was as strong as any feeling I'd ever known. It was as strong as the love I had for Johnny. It was as authentic as the affection I had for Pammy. It was as heartfelt as the concern I had for my mother. I knew that I could not possibly have such passion for someone who did not even exist!"

"That's actually quite insightful, Rebekah."

"My mother died in May of my senior year of high school. Pammy had died at the beginning of that school year. Immediately after my mother died, my father sold our house and moved us into an apartment. Just about two months after my eighteenth birthday, I was married."

Another short, thoughtful pause.

"I guess that I had somehow hoped marrying the fella who had loved me so well would heal all the wounds. I suppose some wounds are never really healed. We just put Band-Aids on them, believing we should—and trying so hard to—hide them from ourselves and everyone else."

Rebekah smiled. "Do you know how long I stayed angry with God? Until my daughter, Lauren, was born. When I held her in my arms for the first time, all I could think about was the miracle I'd been given. I may have very well been angry with Him, but He certainly was neither angry with me nor withholding His love from me simply because I was. That is the God way."

"Why do you believe you held onto the guilt about Pammy?" Dr. Holcomb asked.

"Because I couldn't forgive myself," she answered.

"And now?"

"I still haven't forgiven myself. But in the last couple of weeks, I've embraced a very important truth I heard. One I hadn't allowed myself to consider."

Dr. Holcomb propped an ankle on his other knee. "Really? And what is that?"

"Nowhere in the Bible are we told to forgive ourselves. If we could, or even if we should, there would be no need for a Savior to forgive us. I recently read something similar to this: forgiving ourselves, releasing ourselves of guilt, is found in believing that God has forgiven us through the death and resurrection of His Son, Jesus Christ. How odd that it took me so long to grasp this. To understand it." Rebekah locked eyes with the doctor as a faint smile appeared on both of their faces.

"When is the last time you visited Myrtle Beach?" he asked.

Rebekah tilted her head ever so slightly. "I haven't been back there since Pammy died. Why would I? Why do you ask?"

"I think you should plan a trip down there. I think it would be therapeutic for you."

"I'm not so sure about that." Just the thought unsettled her. "There's nothing there but memories. Memories of all the things that were never meant to be. Shouldn't I focus on the future and not the past?"

"That's a fair question. And yes, by all means, you should focus on the future. What if, though, your future lies in your past? I know that sounds terribly cliché, but often there's good reason why something is cliché, right?"

Rebekah wasn't sure how to answer.

"Just promise me you will think about it. Doctor's orders, if you may."

Rebekah left the appointment without scheduling another. She also left seriously considering his suggestion, although for the life of her, she could not imagine what good could come of it.

But he was the doctor after all, and she had been coming to him for guidance, hadn't she?

Tuesday, May 14, 2024

"Hello, Goodbye"

"What do you want for your birthday this year?"

Her daughter had been asking this same question for several months, and Rebekah knew that with her birthday being exactly one month away she would be asked daily until she gave Lauren an answer.

Rebekah's silence on the subject didn't align with the great thought she'd given the question. Just when she thought she had put Dr. Holcomb's suggestion of visiting Myrtle Beach out of her mind completely, something would happen that would remind her. Even the strange dream she had a few days ago.

It was quite strange indeed. She and Pammy danced on top of a wave while Johnny, Mark, and Mitch sang the Beatles' song, "Hello, Goodbye." Before the song ended, she and Pammy watched as one by one, the boys began sinking into the dark blue ocean water, ever so calmly and ever so peacefully . . . first Johnny and then Mitch and then Mark. Instead of either of the girls panicking or fretting, Rebekah was cognizant of their own peace. She woke up with the same tranquil feeling.

Perhaps a trip to the beach would be good. Perhaps the beach was the perfect place to say goodbye to Johnny properly.

"How about a weekend away at Myrtle Beach? I used to go there all the time as a teenager, and I'd like to show you around."

"Oh, Mother, that sounds like so much fun. A girls' weekend would be perfect."

Rebekah chuckled at how endearing Lauren's "Mother" sounded compared to the snarky way she used the same with her own dear mother. She often wondered how her daughter could be so very different than she was as a teenager. Lauren had never once caused them any trouble or angst. She chuckled to herself again at the thought of that word.

"I think we should go soon. We don't have to wait for the exact day of your birthday," Lauren suggested, breaking into Rebekah's musings. "I just checked ahead for the weather, and it's supposed to be in the mid-eighties. I'm going to book a hotel right now. I'm so excited to be doing this together. And now that Addie is weaned, I can leave her here with her daddy. Or I might bring her. We'll see."

Rebekah hadn't expected so much enthusiasm, but she certainly welcomed it.

As the day of the trip approached, Rebekah found herself having second thoughts though, finding herself between a rock and hard place. Another one of her father's favorite sayings. The meaning of that one, unlike so many of the others, was clear to her from the first time she heard it. Very early on, she felt like she was wrestling her way out of tight spaces with no viable way out. And the day Lauren drove up to get her for their special get-away was yet another example.

She was uneasy about going. Had been for a while. But she couldn't tell Lauren that without some kind of explanation. But how could she even begin to explain any of the reasons to her daughter. Her daughter knew absolutely nothing about her past life except that she had a best friend who had died young. Rebekah had determined that no matter how her own heart ached for what was never to be, she would never let on to her daughter. It was then that she truly understood, for the first time, why her own mother had kept so much from her.

But her mother's secrets didn't include love for another man, even though Rebekah did believe that to be true—for a short period of time, oh so long ago. Neither did her mother's secrets hide the fact that her father wasn't the love of her life.

At any rate, she decided to keep most of her second thoughts to herself, while giving her daughter just a little background, in case she couldn't control her emotions. She was reasonably sure there was a very good possibility of that happening.

Rebekah's stomach began to churn as soon as Lauren drove up. She took a deep breath and greeted her daughter with a hug and a kiss on the cheek. It was a huge relief when her stomach settled, and her nerves calmed within a few minutes. She and Lauren chatted almost nonstop the entire drive.

As they neared the turn-off toward the beach, she felt a surge of excitement thinking about seeing the many places so dear to her heart.

She found herself, however, trying and failing to get her bearings as they approached the strand. "Oh, my, it feels like I've never been here before," she whispered. "Nothing is the same. Silly me, what did I expect?"

"Let's drive along the main road for a bit and see if anything looks familiar," Lauren suggested.

Nothing did.

"I can't tell where things would have been. There were no hotels or condos here back then. The Dairy Queen—we never missed a day with a visit or two there—might have been where those two huge beach houses are." She pointed to her left. "Which means that Rhonda's shop—I really should tell you about Rhonda someday—would have been where the next couple of houses are. But those are all guesses, I have no idea really."

"I'm sorry, Mother. That must make you sad."

"It does. I had hoped to take you to breakfast at the diner." Rebekah became quiet for a few minutes. As she wiped the tear off her cheek, she whispered again, "Silly, silly me."

They drove in silence to the condominium that would be their abode for the weekend. It was beautiful, filled with all the amenities in life Rebekah had grown accustomed to. Amenities and conveniences and most of life's pleasantries had, in fact, been part of her entire married life. The Mark Johnson family never lacked for anything. And if, and only if, the riches that this life often offers could make a person happy—well, then Rebekah would have been the happiest person imaginable.

But she knew that happiness was not to be confused with gratitude and peace. Although she still thought of Johnny often—quite often—she had everything a person could ever ask for in her life with Mark. No one deserved or was guaranteed a trouble-free life, and she was completely aware of the fact that she had more than she could have ever expected.

Once checked in and at their room, Rebekah gazed out over the vast shoreline from their twenty-fourth-floor view off the balcony. "Oh, Lauren, this is a lovely place. You spoil your mother."

"I'm spoiling myself too. I've gotta make a quick phone call, and then I'll come back out and sit with you if you'd like," Lauren told her.

"Of course, I want you to."

She took a seat in one of the two small Rattan chairs. She sat back and scanned the shoreline below. So much had changed. The pier was gone. Not that she had any intention of going out on it, but it saddened her just the same. It saddened her much more so that the pavilion no longer sat where it once did. Had they built another somewhere? Or had that era passed completely?

She thanked God she wasn't there to witness that change. For her, it surely would have been "the day the music died."

Rebekah was humming the Don McLean song "American Pie" when Lauren returned with two glasses of instant Lipton iced tea. Each held a wedge of fresh lemon teetering on the rim of the tall glasses, small enough around for their fingers to touch their thumbs.

"Someone left an unopened jar so I thought we might as well enjoy." Lauren turned to Rebekah with raised glass.

"Cheers." She smiled as her daughter repeated the toast and clinked glasses.

They sat quietly sipping their cold beverages for a while before Rebekah spoke up. "Being here certainly does conjure up the memories."

"I'd love to hear them," Lauren assured her.

"Well, it's crazy how one thought leads to another and then to another. I remember so clearly when a group of us, Pammy and me and a couple of others, walked and walked down the beach just to see where a little white fence separated our beach from what was then called the Colored beach. It was the first time I was exposed to the depth of racism that existed in our country at the time. I was only fourteen or fifteen, but it was a big wake-up call for me that I had been quite sheltered." Rebekah paused, staring at the ocean.

Lauren said nothing. She gave Rebekah the space to reminisce.

Rebekah took a sip of tea. "Anyway, that brought another memory to mind that I just thought of for the first time in a very long time. And it has nothing to do with the beach at all." She paused for a second and continued. "On second thought, I have to say it does. It was here at the beach that I first became aware of the many injustices faced by too many. Somehow, I got it in my head that my parents were part of it all."

After another short pause and then, "Just a couple of days after my mother's funeral, I was in our living room listening to some albums that Pammy and I loved listening to together. I told you about my best friend, Pammy. Do you remember?"

"I do," Lauren answered. "It must have been so hard to go through that."

"It was. I just never could bring myself to talk about it," Rebekah said before she continued with her memory. "The doorbell rang, and I thought a neighbor was stopping by with a casserole, since that was the norm for the first week. When I saw that it was Vonnie Ella I assumed she was there to see my father."

"Who was Vonnie Ella?" asked Lauren.

"She was the black lady who came to our house once a week to do ironing. I started to call out to my father when she touched my arm, stepped inside and hugged me, gently pulling my head to her chest. And I cried for the first time since my bedside goodbye to my mother. She walked me to the couch, held both my hands in hers and told me she was there to see me. I couldn't imagine why she would be there for me. She had brought a lovely picnic basket filled with all my favorite foods. You can just imagine what her beautiful gesture meant to me."

Lauren reached over to take her mother's hand in hers. As her daughter held her hand, Rebekah once again thought about the pearl ring she'd worn on her right ring finger until recently when she replaced the wedding rings on her left hand with it.

"She wanted to tell me my mother had been a good friend to her. That when she was going through difficulties in her family, my mother helped her out. And as much as she appreciated the financial assistance my mother offered, her kindness and friendship meant so much more. And I was so happy to tell her that mama had told me, a few days before she passed, that it was Vonnie Ella who taught her to cook so well. It's funny, Lauren, because I never knew any of that before. In fact, I assumed just the opposite and all these years later, I still don't know why I did that."

Rebekah fell back into deep thought. Once again, Lauren let her process for several minutes.

"I have a good idea, Mother. Let's go down and walk on the beach. The fresh air will be good for both of us."

"Oh . . . what dear? Oh, yes, we should do that. Do you have any idea how many years it's been since I walked on the beach? Well, I might need a calculator to be sure, but let's just say it's been over fifty years. I have to say, I didn't realize how much I missed it."

"I think it's missed you too, and it's been waiting for you." Lauren held Rebekah's hand as they stood and made their way through the condo, down the elevator, across the parking lot and onto the beach.

They quietly walked barefoot along the water's edge for about fifteen minutes. As they turned around to head back, Lauren stopped to face Rebekah. "I think we should make this a tradition. You and me—and Addie because I'm missing her like crazy," she laughed.

"I agree completely. And I miss her too." Rebekah had embraced the joy of grandparenting as soon as she learned of Lauren's pregnancy. She cherished every moment with her darling granddaughter.

The fresh air had been good for her. She was coming to terms with the sadness that would always occupy space in her heart, her mind and her life. But surely, she was not the only one for whom this was true. Probably more so than not.

She had so very much to be thankful for. Her salvation first and foremost. Her marriage to a very good man for many years. Her daughter and granddaughter.

She couldn't quite wrap her head around the fact that, after all these many years, she still thought about Johnny so often. That she still loved him. That he was and always would be her only true love. As badly as it hurt to lose him, she would never regret the time she had with him. She was very blessed indeed to have even known true love at all, and to have the love of her precious family now.

Friday, May 23, 2025

Epilogue

One year later, almost to the day, Rebekah and Lauren—along with Addie—did indeed return to the same beach condo for another girls' weekend. Well, almost all girls. Lauren's husband, Jack, had come along, which was fine with Rebekah because he was most definitely one of her favorite people.

On Saturday morning, Lauren and Addie, now a toddler, frolicked in the water while Rebekah watched from her position on the quilt she made just for such a purpose. She smiled as Addie splashed and laughed and then cried when her face got wet.

Rebekah had continued with Dr. Holcomb for another six months. He had helped so much. She was learning to accept that life was messy and painful. Everyone's mess looked different, and everyone's pain felt different. But it was a common thread, and the longer one lived, the more one faced. At the same time, the longer one lived, the more one grew and learned. Rebekah was grateful she'd learned to let go of the things that dragged life down. And to embrace the many blessings that she'd received along the way.

Rebekah smiled within and without as two of her most precious blessings made their way to her.

"Mother, you just stay here. I'm going to go up to the condo and have Jack put this little wet stinker down for a nap. I'll be right back."

"Oh, well, I can go ahead and come up with you," Rebekah replied. She began to collect her things.

"No, please just wait here. I want to come down and sit here with you and enjoy the sights and sounds together." Lauren wrestled the baby into her arms while wrapping her in a dry towel. "I'll be right back, I promise."

Being at the beach made her both quite happy and somewhat melancholy. The melancholy was taking over as she sat alone. She had to coax her memory to recall the pier where she faced fears and insecurities all alone and spent magical moments with the only boy she ever loved; the dunes where she contemplated life and filled her diaries with her heart's desires and her mind's confusion; and the place where she lost herself in the magic of music, the beloved pavilion.

She embraced the gift of memories. Sometimes, they made her sad; sometimes, they brought her much joy—but they were always hers. Only hers. Memories were another blessing Rebekah would always be thankful for.

She took a long sip from the water bottle beside her, as she zoned in on two young boys throwing a frisbee back and forth. The bright red and purple disc sailed over one of their heads and into the ocean, where a perfectly timed wave scooped it up and carried it out, just out of reach. If they were as blessed as she was, in their old age they would remember that day, that moment, with a mixture of joy and sadness at the carefree life they had.

She shook her head to bring herself from introspection to the present.

Epilogue

Or was she, in fact, in the here and now? Surely not.

As she replaced the water bottle onto the quilt, a sliver of yellow caught her attention. She turned her head to see that what had appeared to be a sliver of yellow was actually a full bouquet of yellow. A bouquet of black-eyed Susans to be exact. She stared, emotionless, and confused, at the beautiful bunch of her favorite flower. Looking up, she saw him.

Yes . . . him. She would have known him anywhere. Never mind that the man who stood smiling at her had a wrinkled face and white hair. Never mind that he seemed a bit shorter and a bit heavier. He was the most handsome man she'd ever seen. Then and now.

She would have known it was him even if he hadn't sat down right beside her and said, "I was just in the neighborhood, is all," as his beautiful green eyes teared up.

After she stared at him for several minutes, she whispered, "Oh, my, I don't understand. I thought you had died." Rebekah's hands shook.

Johnny placed the flowers in her lap and said, "I know. And I'm really sorry about that. By the time I was released from the camp and came home, you had moved. I asked your neighbor, and she told me about your mama. She said that you had gotten married. Broke my heart, Rebekah Sue. But I knew you had no idea what happened to me, and I wasn't about to screw up your happy life."

"What camp?"

"I got captured on a mission. Our whole crew did. Well, the ones who lived through the crash. I was held for three years. I don't talk about it much, but I was pretty messed up for a long time. God has graciously healed me, physically and mentally. And I am eternally thankful. Too many other Vets still suffer from PTSD. I pray for them all the time."

"Oh, Johnny, I am so sorry." She reached out and caressed his cheek. Oh, how she had missed him. After all these years, there they were. Right where it all started. Rebekah suddenly became very self-conscious. "Oh, my. You must be shocked at how old I am now." She removed her hand from his cheek, but he took it in both of his.

"Are you kidding? I just looked for this girl." He pulled the now-faded picture, of her holding up her hand that donned the pearl ring. He smiled and she saw that beautiful smile of his from years ago. His entire face lit up. "Girl, you're the most beautiful thing I've seen in fifty-something years." He held her gaze. He touched the opal ring. "Is this th—?"

Rebekah shook her head as the tears escaped their holding cell. "How is it that you're here? How could you possibly have known that I would be here?"

"Lauren got in touch with me a few months ago. She came across your old diaries and made it her mission to find out the truth about me. Whether or not I died in Viet Nam. And then she made it her mission to get us back together. She's a pretty good sleuth, 'cause here I am."

"I've never forgotten you, Johnny. I've never stopped loving you." Tears rolled down her face now.

"And neither have I, Rebekah Sue. Remember what I wrote when I sent you that ring?"

"Of course, I do. A girl never forgets when a boy proposes to her." She smiled through the tears.

"You remember I said I would do it proper when I saw you? Well, here we are, and that's what I'm doing right now. I never married. I never said these words to anyone else, but I'm saying them to you for the second time. Rebekah Sue, will you marry me?"

Rebekah couldn't speak but she slipped the pearl ring off, placed it back on the ring finger of her right hand and held her left hand out for Johnny to slide the round, brilliant cut diamond in place. He leaned toward her, cupped her chin in his hand and kissed her with the softest, sweetest, and *almost* shortest kiss she had ever received.

"Come on, I've got something to show you." She placed the bouquet down as he stood and held out both of his hands to help her. He handed the bouquet back to her and grabbed the quilt. They made their way to the parking lot where he stopped and told her to look around.

She spotted Lauren, with both hands cupping her tear-stained cheeks, Jack, and in his arms, Addie. And then she saw *it* too. Lauren and Jack were standing right next to it.

"Is it the sa—?"

"The very same. I've kept it in pristine condition. Let's go for a spin, what do ya say?"

"Oh, Johnny, I can't believe it." More tears flooded down her face.

After hugs all around, he held the door as Rebekah slipped in and then made his way to the driver's side. They waved to their small audience, who stood watching them drive away, with the top down, in the 1965 powder blue Mustang.

Post Epilogue

In the distance—unseen by human eyes, unheard by human ears—was another audience altogether.

Susan, Rhonda, Vonnie Ella, and Big John stood cheering Rebekah and Johnny on. And they would be there again when the wedding bells begin to ring . . .

Forget not to show love unto strangers: for thereby some have entertained angels unawares.
—Hebrews 13:2

Acknowledgments

Although this book has been in my heart and mind for years, in many and various forms, it absolutely would not have been written if not for the wonderful support and input from three people who gave of their time and encouragement from the moment I asked.

Thank you, Savanna, for your proofreading and suggestions very early on in this book writing process—all while pursuing your master's degree. You have always had and always will have my heart.

Thank you, Linda and Jessica, for your wonderful encouragement and input. Thanks for taking the time and energy to read and comment on the entire manuscript; that means more than you can possibly know.

To my editor, Tracy Wainwright, thank you for all of your hard work and for understanding what I wanted to say and making it beautiful.

Many thanks to Lucid Books for the incredible job they have done in publishing this book as well as my memoir. God brought Lucid to me, and He always brings the best. I honestly cannot thank the Lucid team enough for making this journey possible.

You are all a part of *Entertaining Angels*.

Scan for the playlist inspired by this book.

www.ingramcontent.com/pod-product-compliance
Lightning Source LLC
Chambersburg PA
CBHW060501090426
42735CB00011B/2065